JOURNEY OF A DEVELOPMENT WORKER

SHUN-ICHI MURATA
Kwansei Gakuin University Press

Shun-ichi Murata

University Professor of International Relations,
Focal Point for "Conflict Analysis and Its Aid Policy" at School of Policy Studies,
Kwansei Gakuin University, Kobe-Sanda Campus, Japan
Visiting Lecturer for United Nations University's Global Seminar in 2003
Obtained degrees from
Kwansei Gakuin University, Hyogo, Nishinomiya, Japan
George Washington University, Washington, D.C., USA
Harvard University - Kennedy School of Government, Cambridge, USA

Journey of a Development Worker

Copyright © 2003 by Shun-ichi Murata
First edition published 1999 as "FOOTPATHS and HIGHWAYS" Revised edition published 2003.

All rights reserved.

No part of this book may be reproduced in any form or by any means without permission in writing from the author.

The views expressed herein are those of the author and do not necessarily reflect the views of the United Nation Development Program.

Kwansei Gakuin University Press
1-1-155 Uegahara, Nishinomiya, Hyogo, 662-0891, Japan
Cover design by Michiko Matsushita
ISBN:4-907654-47-2

To Hiroko, Keiichiro
and
development workers everywhere

TABLE OF CONTENTS

Introduction		1
Chapter 1:	From Hometown to Crossroads	3
Chapter 2:	Uganda: Baptism by The Lake, Marriage and Escape	19
Chapter 3:	The Companion Arrives	36
Chapter 4:	Uphill Fights	46
Chapter 5:	China of My Dreams	51
Chapter 6:	Rough Road	69
Chapter 7:	A New Landscape Awaits	91
Chapter 8:	Trouble in Paradise	115
Chapter 9:	One Glance Backward, One Step Forward	130
Chapter 10:	Open at Peril, Stay Close and Die	155
Chapter 11:	Mindanao Revisited	165
Chapter 12:	A Better Map for Changing Terrain	175
Chapter 13:	Homeland and New Horizons	189
Appendix	緊急援助と開発協力のはざまから―開発ワーカーのディレンマ	193

INTRODUCTION

Complex, twisting, often exhausting, occasionally life-threatening; nevertheless, always highly interesting and deeply fulfilling.

Such is the road all development practitioners have walked, and as I make my own journey, I can say in all honesty, *I would not have it any other way.* I have always wanted to build a bridge between this road and the roads that so many other people may be traveling—even life paths that may seem decidedly far removed from development work, but which are, nonetheless, influenced or (hopefully) benefited by it.

When I first set out to write of my lifework—*Footpaths & Highways,* what is actually the first edition of this book—I had in mind, despite the limited number of copies initially printed, the most varied readership possible....

Students still in the process of defining what course they ultimately wanted to take. Women, whose energies were fully devoted to balancing roles as partner, parent, income earner, caregiver, household manager. Young professionals seeking to find, or perhaps wanting to infuse, meaning and substance in their chosen careers. People in their own midlife crossroads, their spirits searching for more ways to leave indelible legacies to future generations.

It has been three years since *Footpaths & Highways* was released. Since that time so many things have taken place, and some come to my mind with particular immediacy and clarity: the first ever television broadcast in the Bhutanese capital of Thimphu; the swift and highly charged turn of events in Mindanao, Philippines which have occasionally threatened to overshadow or even undo some of the hard-won gains in of the UN-backed peace and development plan; the deep and massive economic downturn in Japan, an oft-predicted scenario that nonetheless devastated millions of Japanese who had always banked on lifelong-jobs and substantial savings.

It was my hope then, and it is still my desire now, as I share with you this *Journey of a development worker,* that in the pages to follow you shall find inspiration, encouragement, or even compelling reasons for taking up, or continuing, or supporting development work. Whatever corner of the world you may be making your own mark in. Whatever you may have envisioned your life to be.

Because ultimately, all our roads intersect in this world, and development—wherever and however it takes place—makes all our journeys a little lighter, and all our destinations closer and better.

Shun-ichi Murata
2002

CHAPTER 1

FROM HOMETOWN TO CROSSROADS

Anywhere, everywhere. For as long as there are people there.

Simple words, spoken at that time in 1980, when I really did not have any particular destination in mind. Those simple words surprised Frederick Lyons, currently Resident Representative of UNDP Kenya, and then United

Nations Development Programme recruiting officer—and a veteran at grilling recruits in what may be the most diverse human resource pool in the world. It seemed to be the first time he had heard such an answer. He smiled.

Neither of us could have guessed the rich rewards that that simple answer would bring me. However, even as a youngster, I had already known how simple things have a way of giving great fulfillment.

One of the first places I learned that was in my hometown of Yukuhashi, Fukuoka,Kyusyu Island, in Japan. Although it was really a city, and near the bustling area of Nagasaki with its Chinese and Korean communities, its traders and its thinkers, my hometown was nevertheless a very small city. I grew up there in the late 1950's, when ours was the kind of neighborhood where the playground had no fence. It had no walls. Instead it had lines of cherry and plum blossom trees. Our summer swimming pool was a deep lake surrounded by soft, low green-covered hills. There was also a nearby forest that held other treats like horseback riding or hiking.

Within the town itself, I found plenty of opportunities for both simple fun and mischief. Japanese children being generally subdued, I was quite a peculiar child in my parents' eyes, active and naughty, unlike my more behaved elder brother. In my five-year-old world, the many merchant shops in our community was paradise.

At the grocery store, I would pick fruits to take home with me. One time I tried to sneak out a whole bunch of bananas in my pocket. I also had the habit of sneaking out the best cakes at the bakery—the same bakery which I had once thrown stones at in an impish fit. I also hung around a small shop selling traditional Japanese clothing. And at the butcher's shop, my kindergarten classmate (the owner's son) was my favorite friend.

Of course most of the shopkeepers knew what I was doing. Generally lenient, they scolded or warned me whenever necessary. They'd go, "Shun-ichi, what are you doing?" "Shun-ichi, don't do that!"
"That was not good, Shun-ichi!!!" Or, all else failing, they would spank me.

It was that kind of community where people knew each other by first name. And neighbors took care of each other's children.

They knew if I would be spending the day at a certain place, or spending the night with a neighbor's child, and they weren't bothered, although once or twice they would ask, "Where has Shun-ichi gone to this time?" Still, they knew me, they knew my parents, and they had been given the right, the privilege, the pain of helping raise me up, and all other children as well. Perhaps they only saw me more often than the others, because I was always running and moving and hanging around the neighborhood.

They were also very familiar with me because our family had one of the town's very first television sets (In 1950's, TV set is not popular or widely spread in Japan). Our relatively small household always swelled in number during daytime, what with the neighbors freely going in and out of the house to glimpse a show or sit down and watch with us.

Meanwhile, my parents were busy with the family business, a trading firm that my father's father used to own.

My father, Tetsuji, had been a soldier, taken right out of college during the conscription of World War II. During the war, his aircraft carrier was sunk near the Philippine seas. Trying to return to college after the war, he found the school and his former life completely gone. So he took over the trading and retailing firm instead, and ran it with the help of my mother.

My father was the second son in a large family of landowners and politicians, a clan that had formerly been among the noble "samurai" class. The end of the war and agrarian reform took away both the noble title and much of the land and properties. What remained was a handful of lots, and the high quality of education they had received. While my mother, Yoko, helped my father in managing the firm, her other relatives were involved in either the teaching or the medical field.

It was not surprising, therefore, that I developed a fascination for the life of Albert Schweitzer, whose story I had read when I was ten. Just the right age to dream and be inspired.

And what better man to inspire me then than this German? An authority on Bach, an accomplished performer of Bach's organ music, and a respected German theologian, who in a mid-career change, took up medicine, and thereafter spent the rest of his life building and running a hospital in what is now Gabon in equatorial Africa.

My fascination—not just with his personal life, but the kind of committed service that such a life required—grew immensely with the influence of my mother's cousin, Dr. Akira Kobayashi, who would later become one of Japan's top surgeons.

He came to visit us sometime when I was thirteen. He had completed his studies abroad, and journeyed to the United Kingdom, France, and several African and Asian countries, observing the medical situation in those places.

During his visit, we spent much time talking about his trips. He told many stories of doctors working in developing countries. Young as I was, he tried to make me understand what he had seen and gone through, and what he had hoped to do.

"We must always find room in our lives to help others," he insisted. "We need to help other people, especially those in the poorer countries, those in the developing world. We have to do that, if we want to have peace in this world, if we want order in this world."

As I listened, I thought of going to China. I had read about it, known how near it was to my own country, heard about it from those who had been in the war, and learned about its people firsthand from a young Chinese friend I had. Despite my deep interest in Albert Schweitzer's life, it did not occur to me to try out my cousin's prescription for world peace by going to Africa.

Hearing of my relative's tales, though, and thinking about Albert Schweitzer's lifework, made me think of Babe Ruth.

In Japan, the popularity of such traditional sports like *judo*, *kendo*, and *sumo* wrestling, does not in any way diminish the wide-spread acceptance of imports like baseball.

So at that young age, I, too, was hooked on Babe Ruth. What struck me most about him was his charisma. He made people—he made me—believe he could always do more. Always better than his last performance. And better than any other baseball player.

His was the infectious, inspiring kind of superhuman commitment that I felt was needed in something as difficult and important as the work which Schweitzer and my cousin's peers were doing.

Unfortunately, while humanitarian work was slowly shaping up to become a personal mission for me, the foundation that was supposed to launch me on such a career—my education—was wobbly, at best.

And all because I was determined to continue enjoying life while studying.

My attitude was tantamount to being anarchic when you consider how, from as far back as Japan's feudal age, education has been very serious business for the Japanese. The modern national education system was set up in 1872. Compulsory education was made free of charge in 1900. And in the years following World War II, several relevant laws were passed that set the pace for today's Japanese school systems.

What was true then and now was the kind of work required of students, more so in the public schools, which were more demanding than the private schools.

Even in a town as small as ours, the public school was known for its high standards.

Still, I began well enough, passing examinations without studying as hard, or as often, or as consistently as the others. I eventually became a quick-fix expert when it came to reviews and tests. By the time I reached senior high school, though, everyone else simply studied harder, and more often, and even more consistently. I was forced to catch up.

Maybe I didn't catch up fast enough. By the time I was ready to leave high school, I was cautioned by our counselor, Mr. Togo, against applying at a first-class medical school. He was not being unduly pessimistic. University entrance exams are notoriously difficult. Japanese students often need to add to their regular study load and attend preparatory school classes (*juku* or *yobiko*) on weekends and weekday evenings just to increase their chances.

Hurt by my counselor's advice, and certain that I could make it, I applied. Sure enough I failed. I had to make a complete change of direction in the entrance exam, from medical school to social science.

My advantage was that I was quite good in math and statistics, so I didn't have to study so hard in Japanese history, as my elective entrance examination was mathematics. But I was still very much caught in a dilemma, the outcome of which would direct the course of the rest of my life.

My parents took me aside and told me pointblank: "You should think more seriously about your own life."

"Where do you want to go? Are you going to be a doctor?"

"Forget about it," I said.

I had decided to put my medical dreams on hold in the meantime. I was more concerned with the many choices available in the social science field. I wondered which one I should go to.

I finally settled on law and political science, considering its applicability to any field, even medicine. Other social sciences like economics struck me as not being too flexible. Besides, I thought, in the law field, I could engage with people directly, just like in the medical field.

So I took the test, passed, and entered Kwansei Gakuin University near Kobe in Hyogo Prefecture in the Kinki region. It was among the top ten school in Japanese universities?

This time, I couldn't study much—not really out of choice, but out of circumstance. I had come into the university right before the students went on strike. But I had fun, because that was the period dominated by Marxists, and it was the fashion to study the Marxist economy. I was part of a so-called Neo-Marxist group, as far as ideology went. Yet our main concern was really to study why there was so much inequality and lack of development in many areas of the world. This was actually when my involvement with development work started in the scholarly context.

While the regular class was shut down because the students were on strike, I was becoming engrossed with underdevelopment and the disparity between the rich and the poor countries.

It was also at Kwansei Gakuin that I had my first, albeit limited, involvement, with international relations: I was a president of our student association, "The English Speaking Society (E.S.S.)"—for "Volunteers in Asia".

That post was not just a title for me. It was a chance to do something. I put my energies into creating a standard orientation program for foreign volunteers. Before entering their host countries, these Stanford University student volunteers were given pertinent, face-saving pointers on eating habits, living standards, and the like.

I also found myself being deeply involved in the university's English Club.

Strangely, as president of that club, I was an object of interest for many of my female club members. (The others, more predictably, were simply not interested, thank you.) For my part, I was seriously dating someone, someone with whom I had plans of getting engaged and later marrying. Nevertheless, that didn't stop me from clearly remembering an incident involving one of the club members, Hiroko Satsuma, a warm and friendly young lady whom I was starting to like.

It was one of those ordinary rainy days, the kind when you put on your raincoat rather absentmindedly, not caring enough to notice that a button or two might be missing.

As soon as I reached the university, I bumped into Hiroko. Without much fuss or explanation, she whipped out a sewing kit from her handbag and quickly, deftly sewed a button onto my raincoat. I was shocked. Here was somebody who truly spoke without words; who expressed caring in such a simple, unselfconscious act. I thought it was a strikingly, disarmingly traditional way of expressing sentiment—through action and behavior, not through words.

Yet there remained the fact that I was seriously seeing someone.

So I completed my law studies by 1976, and for two years became preoccupied with my work as campaign organizer for the Liberal Democratic Party in Kitakyushu.

The next crossroads opened up for me courtesy of one of our university professors, Professor "A".

He told me, "Look closely at the international gap between economies. Study how that gap can be reduced. And learn why we are responsible for that."

He also urged me to go abroad for further study.

"Go to the United States or the United Kingdom....Go to the so-called nests of capitalism and colonialism. You can choose one of them. Then you can understand better how those people rule the world."

In 1978, I was able to follow the Professor's advice. I got a scholarship to George Washington University, and entered its Institute of Sino-Soviet Studies, where I completed my master course in International Politics, and went on to the doctor program.

I had purposely chosen the locale: Washington, D.C. was, after all, the mecca of international politics, the perfect place to get a fresh and close up view of how the politicians run the world's affairs. It was also there that I experienced the difficulties of adjusting; in particular, I was finding it hard to communicate. It was so bad that unless I really improved my English skills, I could not possibly hope to graduate from that school. My American peers and friends rose to the occasion, however, and their efforts proved to be more persistent than my language problem.

Having accomplished all these, I felt I was ready to embark on a teaching career, and settle down with the lady I was engaged to, "Ms. K". It was not to be, however. For some reason she suddenly didn't want to marry me anymore. I later found out she had run away with my best friend.

I was hanging in the air! I didn't know what to do anymore. I had lost half of my life's direction because I had no more reason to go back to Japan. After all, she was Japanese and I had always thought I was going to spend my life there with her.

With our engagement ended so abruptly, I had not only become uncertain of my future. I had also become unsure as to what role to take in the development arena. Up until then, I had been thinking of my development role mainly in terms of teaching, and inspiring students to make their contribution to society. I never thought about becoming a development practitioner. I was not thinking that way at all.

Again, it was one of my university professors, Dr. Young Kim, who showed me the way.

He asked me if I was interested in doing graduate school internship in New York. Since the university would pay for it, I agreed, partly as a way of forgetting my emotional problems.

So off I was to the United Nations. At the professional recruitment services and secretariat, I met Mr. Shigeo Iwai, the Japanese recruitment officer, who asked me, "Why don't you just fill out the form for junior professional officer's program?"

He explained that it was a scheme sponsored by the Japanese ministry of foreign affairs. I was not very keen on it. Highly critical of United Nations policies around the world, I was not interested in working directly in the system because I wanted to complete my mission of teaching students. So I was really facing a dilemma.

My response actually boiled down to running away from everything.

I said to myself that at least I had two years to cool down and think. I signed, took the examinations, and later went through the interview.

After the examinations (which included language examinations), the interview was the most difficult part. Mine was conducted by the recruitment officer in the United Nations Development Programme (UNDP). I didn't know whether I was going to the UNDP, UNICEF, UNFPA, or any other UN organization. The Japanese permanent mission recruitment officer, Mr. Tsuneo Fujiwara, asked me to apply with the UNDP. Again, I agreed, this time without any idea of what the UNDP was doing. My primary motivation was still very much tied to my fiancee's "departure".

My decision to join the UNDP was something my parents never thought of or expected. Perhaps they had already resigned themselves to an aimless, unclear future for their happy-go-lucky youngest. They had become tired of telling me what to do, giving advice and suggestions that I never listened to or followed anyway.

Understandably, they were shocked when I told them about it.

It was not only something totally unpredictable on my part. It was also something rare in the United Nations' ranks at that time. Japan had entered the UN in 1956, just three years after I was born. It had gone into Official Development Assistance in 1975 after several decades of rehabilitating the nation first. Prior to the establishment of the junior professional officers program, the country simply did not have enough human resources to spare, as most citizens already had their hands full with national reconstruction work. At that time, international organizations were also, for the most part, unknown territory.

There were about 110 Japanese professionals working in the whole UN system in those days. The UN secretariat had almost 3000 professionals; the UNDP, about 800—and exactly 12 were Japanese.

And most of the Japanese were not necessarily engaged in policy but in the service arena: recruitment services, personnel services. Very few were directly involved in development practice. That's why in the university, in the Japanese society where I had grown, and even in the big city that Tokyo was, Japanese development professionals were rare, very rare.

But there I was in 1980, fresh from my internship which had lasted from June to July; a twenty-six-year-old recruit with a blank blueprint for the future. However, I had done some homework, and felt relaxed as I faced Mr. Lyons, the recruiting officer.

"Mr. Murata, where would you like to go? Do you have any preference regarding where you want to go?"

"I can go anywhere, everywhere. For as long as there's people there, people who need me."

Surprised yet unfazed, he pressed on.

"So do you want to go to Uganda or Thailand?"

Once more, I told him I was prepared to go anywhere. "As long as there are people living there, there must be something I can do. I've nothing to lose."

"Wouldn't you like to go to maybe Paris or London?"

he offered.

Anywhere, came my consistently noncommittal reply.

"How about Chad?" he said.

"Are there people there?"

It was the only thing I wanted to know.

Not long after, the letter came: "We are delighted to tell you that you have been accepted by the UNDP." Within two weeks I was asked to go to Bhutan. I didn't know where it was, so I looked it up, saw it was on the upper part of India, just the northern portion, and seeing it, saw a tiny, tiny kingdom which seemed very interesting, indeed. I was excited.

But then in two weeks the Resident Representative of Uganda had changed the course of action, so I was asked to go to Uganda instead.

Many people—myself and my family included—were still not aware of where Uganda was back then. My parents knew where Africa was, but at the time they had been educated, most of those countries were colonized by either the French or the English. I said, Uganda sounds like east Africa. My parents, knowing why I had joined the UNDP, felt disposed to help me cope, so they gave their blessings, saying, "Why don't you give it a try—maybe only two weeks?"

So on November 3, I officially joined the UNDP, and set my sights on my assignment in Uganda, armed only with three things: the collection of horror stories which some UN staff had helpfully shared; descriptions of a beautiful country from other UN staff; and my own open mind that chose to suspend judgment until after I got there.

CHAPTER 2

UGANDA: BAPTISM BY THE LAKE, MARRIAGE AND ESCAPE

As I was preparing for my first assignment, Uganda was busy sorting out its own affairs.

Milton Obote, who had previously ruled the rich, rugged country for almost 11 years, had returned to power a year after his usurper, Maj. Gen. Idi Amin Dada, had been driven out by the combined efforts of Tanzanian and Ugandan exiles.

Deeply scared by the terrors of Idi Amin's rule, the country was finding it hard to start again. There was chaos still. Inflation was incredible. The price of one bottle of Coca Cola was equivalent to a senior secretary's salary for one month. Corruption and misappropriation of funds were commonplace, even in the UN office itself. It was a daily problem.

All the people's concerns boiled down to survival.

My own pressing concern was how to arrive at my posting in one piece.

I used the southern route: from Tokyo airport, first stop Singapore, next stop Karachi. It was at the Swiss Air Terminal in Karachi that I noticed that my luggage was not going to Uganda but to Zurich. An announcement from the flight attendant confirmed it: "Unfortunately, your luggage may be going to Zurich." I found out that there had been some mistake, specifically Swiss Air's. There was apparently nothing anyone could do. I would actually be reunited with my baggage three months later. In the meantime, I was proceeding with my flight in an extreme case of traveling light.

Also at Karachi, no announcement had been made regarding our flight. I got off at two o'clock in the morning, barely making it to the airplane.

Next stop was Nairobi airport for the connecting flight to Uganda. Without foreign currency to purchase jet fuel, Uganda Air could not arrange for the connecting flight. All the passengers were stuck. I asked around, "Does this happen often?"

"Oh yes, this is a regular thing," they assured me.

"What is the flight schedule?"

It didn't matter; it was never followed.

I spent another day in Nairobi. Usually the airport takes care of the hotel accommodations for stranded passengers. But they had no money. I had to take care of myself. Finally, the connecting flight was provided.

UGANDA: BAPTISM BY THE LAKE, MARRIAGE AND ESCAPE

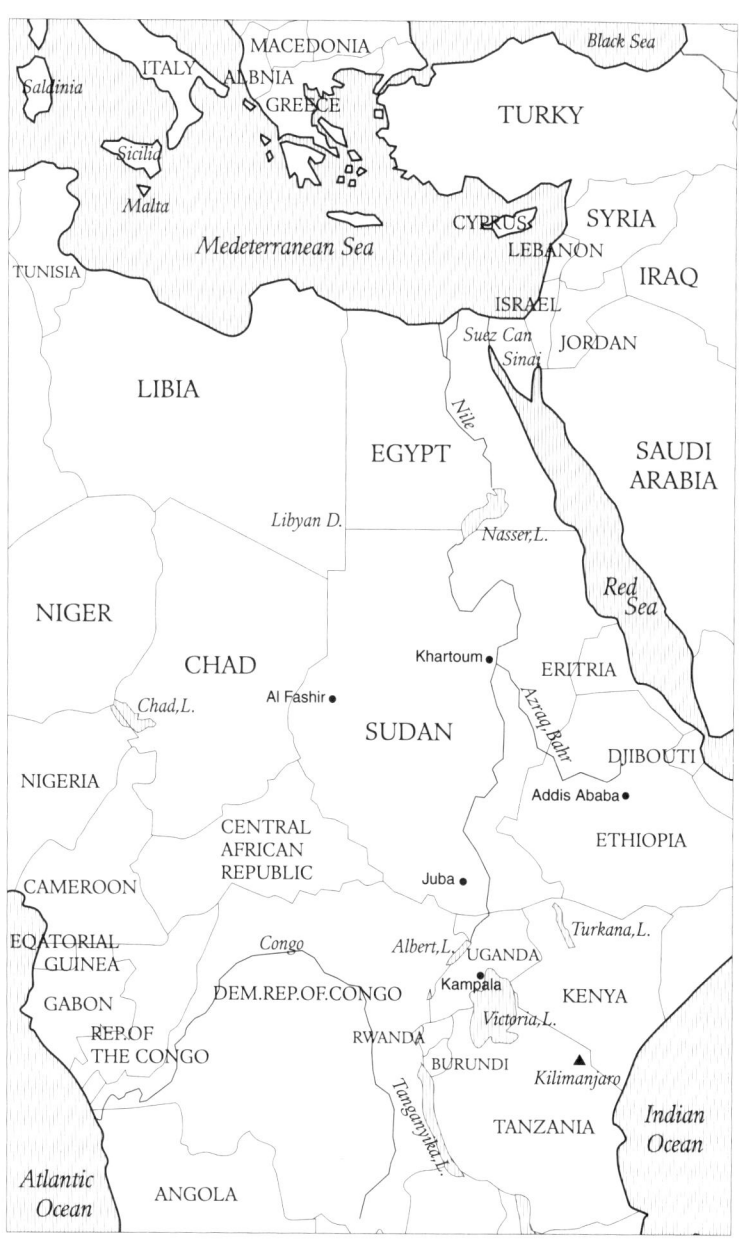

The airplane was a Fokker friendship—a reliable airplane—yet I was so afraid of what could happen.

Passengers had to hand-carry their own luggage because there was no conveyor belt. Good thing I had no luggage. There were laborers willing to carry the luggage but the passengers had no money, either. I saw some passengers put the bags in the compartments and I mistook them for baggage boys. In the cockpit, there was just the pilot. No copilot. And just one flight attendant. They made up the entire crew. I got on the airplane and later, as we were landing, I looked out to the landing strip. I was reminded of the raid on Entebbe. We landed there. I was finally on Ugandan soil, ready to begin my life as a UNDP junior professional officer.

The UNDP, however, was not ready. No one came to pick me up. I noticed later on that someone from UNDP had come to pick up my pouch. The pouch was more important.

No less than 42 kilometers separate Entebbe from the capital, Kampala. There were no taxi services—nor much infrastructure, for that matter—because of the turmoil. There were illegal taxi services, though, so I rode a black market taxi. My fare amounted to fifty dollars. I thought it amounted to a holdup. Then I proceeded to the UNDP office in downtown Kampala. On my way, there were a lot of roadblocks, machine guns, sporadic shooting, bursts of gunfire. I'm in the middle of war, I thought. Finally, arriving at the UNDP office unharmed, I discovered that my name was not on the visitors' roll.

The receptionist apologized, and I introduced myself and informed her of my assignment. I next spoke to the supervisor, and he said my name was not there, there must be a mistake.

I replied, of course, that I was not mistaken, I was quite certain I was expected there. So I was introduced to the Deputy Resident Representative there, a Dutchman, Dirk Hylkema.

"Welcome to Uganda," he said. "How did you come here?"

I said I just took a black market taxi.

"I sent someone to pick you up and the pouch."

I said that they picked up the pouch but they forgot about me. So he shook my hand: "Welcome to Africa. This is the way it is. I went through exactly the same thing when I arrived here." Then I was introduced to everybody.

The next order of battle was to find myself a set of clothes. Because of the crisis, there were understandably very few they could spare, and even fewer that were my size. I was wearing the same clothes for almost three weeks until some souls got very sympathetic and gave me trousers. Then people thought that I was some kind of officer.

Housing was another problem. I was fortunate enough to share a big colonial house with one Swiss lady, Ms. Ruth Honegger, who was running a trading company there. She was a very attractive lady, so rumor spread that there was some kind of cohabitation with me. However, she also happened to be the girlfriend of the World Food Program coordinator. That made the story more complicated. The man in question, though, did not really mind. He himself was going out with a number of other ladies.

This was not merely a dating game, though. It was part of a deeper need to make sure that they were all still alive despite what was happening around. Everyday tension was so high that when night came, it was the least comfort you could have—to be with somebody, whether it was for the simple presence of another human being, or for sex. It was a uniquely difficult time to try and do normal work, accomplish the immense reconstruction needed, while trying to stay alive. I found it all very, very disturbing.

Shooting was going on; it was not long before I experienced seeing people being gunned down in front of me in the street fighting. Going to the office everyday meant driving ourselves through the few pockets of quiet in between the exchange of bullets. In my capacity as deputy to the UN security officer, I had to look out for myself, and for the other UN personnel as well.

One time the Indian High Commission, which belonged to the cluster of offices where ours was located, was bombed. The gasoline station was also bombed. We saw all these from our building. And all the while, the ground was shaking in what felt like a magnitude 7 earthquake. Twice, things got so bad, we were evacuated to Kenya. But the UN was strongly committed to Uganda. At that time, there was no other major group working there.

Tragically, all this chaos was happening in what is arguably one of the loveliest, most richly-endowed nations in Africa. The former British protectorate was in fact a favorite retirement destination of the colonizers.

This landlocked plateau sitting some 3,000 to 5,000 feet above sea level is generously nourished by freshwater lakes and swamps. Its elevation gives it its relatively mild climate, considering it straddles the equator. There are thickly forested areas near the Ruwenzori Mountain range to the country's west, and the fertile red soil is responsible for quality coffee, fruit and grain produce, and cotton for export.

Uganda had a lot going for it. It was a matter of calming the country's troubled spirit, and rebuilding the critical infrastructure through which the nation's economic lifeblood could once again flow.

So I found myself, at 27 years old, on my first UNDP posting, with 30 project assignments. Several of these had to be shut down later because of the security risk; there were, however, three that pushed through.

These most active ones were very interesting.

For one, there was the rehabilitation of the Lake Victoria Hotel, which was the UN residence at that time. Close to the Entebbe airport, the hotel badly needed work before it could accommodate visitors.

I had zero knowledge of the hotel business. I had no choice but to take an on-the-job crash course in everything: writing, catering, occupancy rates, cost benefit analysis and advising. I even had to train people, and bring in a Swiss hotel management group for that purpose.

There was, again, controversy in the Lake Victoria Hotel.

It involved the UN system's senior official—and the official's spouse. The official was engaged in the management of the hotel.

So was the spouse. The result of the arrangement was actually mismanagement, with the spouse involved in a lot of things regarding the hotel operations, including bidding procedures that ranged from the controversial to the downright questionable. I was caught in between.

All this made the Lake Victoria project's operational and administrative activities very, very complicated. I had to keep figuring out the extent of my responsibility and accountability. The spouse was, of course, accountable, yet at the same time, not directly or officially responsible.

I was nearing the edge. I feared being used as a scapegoat.

Fortunately, it was not long before the official left. Immediately afterwards, I organized an evaluation mission so that I could thoroughly investigate and make an official documentation that I was not directly involved in it.

We terminated the project, and the Swiss hotel administration group took over. Fortunately for them it was a lucrative project. Everyone had to pay in hard currency. It also had a virtual monopoly of the hotel industry there.

My work in the hotel was finished. It was time to work in the village.

I was tasked with field research work in a community of the Karamojon nomads. The results were to be turned over to the operational organizations like the World Food Program and UNICEF, as basis for their livelihood project planning.

These nomads live in the northern part of Uganda, close to the Sudanese border. Although a minority group, the Karamojons are critical in the political stability of Uganda. Armed, fierce, the Karamojons were to be my hosts for the next few weeks, and the subject of my study.

The day I arrived at one of the largest Karamojon communities, the chieftain was there, and I was told to take all my clothes off. Everyone else was naked. And young healthy men, in particular, were proud to be naked.

They were also very curious about me. I was not white. I was not black. I was a Japanese—the very first one they met.

So I took my clothes off. Not everything, anyway, explaining that if I took off everything, and marched together with them, I was going to burn everywhere. My driver, who was from that tribe, helped translate and negotiate for me. I could not get away with everything, however. I had to leave my car and march with them to the village proper—practically one hundred kilometers away. This was through a stretch of savanna; heat and brightness everywhere, broken here and there by low trees and plants.

Once there, it was time to eat. The first food that came to my mind was meat, the Karamojons being cattle growers. True enough, there was cattle. But no cow was to be killed in my honor. Instead, they cut a little piece from the head of the cow, let the blood drip into a small cup, mixed it with milk, and drank the mixture.

Apart from that, they had porridge made of cassava. They ate fruit when it was available, which was very rare. But they survived with that mixture as their staple food. To me, though, in that hot climate, the taste was challenging, to say the least. I threw up at my first taste. It took me two days to get adjusted to it. I was trapped many times by things like those. And it was always my driver who talked them into pardoning or excusing me.

The community itself was simple, and primitive; dangerous, yet fascinating. Some time before I arrived, a German volunteer had also gone there. He had not come back alive. About 1,000 males—many of them armed—were marching around. The females usually settled somewhere else. There was no electricity, only water, and even that was scarce. They pumped out the water from a nearby stream and a common well.

Within a week after I arrived, I fell ill with malaria. It had actually been in my blood even before I had gone to the village; it is just like the flu in Africa. You catch it, you survive it—it was not the fearsome disease that other countries fussed about. There were, of course, people who did die from it. But I had it so many times there. Later on,

I had to take chromium phosphate—actually a poison, which affected my eyes and my liver for a long time. But I didn't immediately know how bad my first bout was, because I was strong. Until one day, I just couldn't hold my balance while standing. My hosts tried giving me the local cure. It looked like dried papaya, though I couldn't tell what it was exactly. It didn't work very well, though.

Despite the malaria attacks, I stayed there for a full month. I lived, ate, slept there; we joked, I asked questions, discovered something almost daily. In due time, their deep and instinctive mistrust of outsiders gave way to friendship. It was not a quick or easy process, of course. They had never seen a Japanese, let alone heard of Japan. They also did not understand what the UN was. The only way I could reach out was to demonstrate my sincerity, to show that I was there to help. Again, my driver was largely responsible for bridging the language gap.

We also gave them emergency food supplies, and seeds and plows, so they could at least engage in livelihood activities. In return, they gave me the information I needed: the pattern of their movements, the basics of their culture, the reasons for conflict, their motives for attacking other tribes or other clans.

I found out that cattle raiding was often the spark. In the past, whenever the marriage season came, the men would kill the lions to demonstrate how strong they were. But there were no more lions by the time I was there. So if a young person were to get married, instead of killing a lion to demonstrate to the group how strong he was (and make them think they could get rich), he would raid the cattle of other clans. In so doing he created a bond between his clan and that of his future wife. The raiding produced a cycle of retaliation. It became clear to me that as far as the Karamojon were concerned, the security problem did not concern the government. The war was all about cattle raiding.

In those weeks, I had learned the slow, painstaking process of confidence-building. I never realized how much patience was needed. I also did not realize how deeply they valued my friendship until I completed my research.

Then I was offered the chieftain's two daughters in marriage.

It was a most difficult position. My driver said if I refused, I would almost certainly never get out of there. They were going to cut me into pieces, because it was an insult to the chieftain. If I said yes, the two daughters would come with me wherever I went.

I explained that I would come back again to make the arrangements possible. In the negotiation process, I had to leave with them a gold chain bracelet I had as a sign that I was going back. They didn't need paper money because they didn't trust anyone. They only needed gold.

And I only needed to escape.

There was more work to be done. Upon my return to Kampala, I was put in charge of the Entebbe airport improvement and rehabilitation. The airport was the lifeline of the area, the gateway to the capital. My primary concern was air safety. The airport had, until then, been relying on visual landings. Radar-assisted landings were unheard of.

As with the hotel industry, I had to start from square one, and cover as much ground as I could in aircraft technology, air safety, air transport management, and airport equipment.

It was there that I got the chance to work with Japanese technicians. I represented the UN as the funding agency, and they were the executing agency assigned. They were members of an international civil aviation organization (the Japan Radio Corporation or Nihon Musen). The bidding committee found their credentials best suited to our requirements. After putting in place the radar-guided landing system, we worked to increase the aircraft and the airstrip's capacity. Often, we had to open the airport 24 hours in order to improve and ensure the inflow and outflow of supplies and passengers. The UNDP took the lead in all this with the assistance of representatives from the United States, the United Kingdom, the Netherlands, and other major European countries. The UN was covering up to 40 percent of the entire assistance grant. The United States provided the largest country donation.

Nevertheless, for the most part of those turbulent years in Africa, the US and other countries' bilateral assistance was very supply-driven. The donor countries decided in behalf of the beneficiaries in terms of the kind of assistance needed.

The other donors gave supplies, relief, and other forms of help. The UN made it a point to stay with the people.

Sadly, too, there was a lot of material assistance that came in the form of expired medicines, obsolete equipment, and similarly unacceptable "aid". For a long time, Africa was being used as a dumping ground of sorts by the industrialized countries. To a certain extent, it's still happening now.

At that point, I was also concerned about the instability of the recipient government, particularly the depth and extent of the corruption among the leaders. I was also not naive enough to be blind to the corruption even among the UN officers, and the quality of some of the "experts".

In two short years I had passed crossroad after crossroad. Directly engaging in the operations in Uganda opened my eyes to diverse paths. I could not close my eyes. What were supposed to be avenues for solutions became channels for more problems. Development assistance was benefiting the industrialized nations more, and the quality of the human resources we had was far below what I expected.

I felt the best recourse—the best way to resist and protest—was to leave.

On the other hand, I could clearly see there was so much more that needed to be done. I recognized that Uganda and the other African countries' independence came into the picture only in the 1960s, and I was there in 1981. In those years, had I been asking too much in expecting them to develop and catch up with the rest of the world? Wasn't there anything (within the duration of the project) that they could have done that could have molded them to develop faster? I was sensitive to the reality that Japan's own supposedly miraculous recovery took about 30 years.

The thought of the development work that actually remained to be accomplished was a compelling factor for me. For one, I saw that in many of our societies, specialization had become a skill, a prized goal, making us forget other talents and potentials. In places like Uganda, what kind of specialization could we do? We could not be that limited.

All that time, I was able to explore myself, what talents I may be able to use. At the same time this ability to explore was, in itself, sharpened.

Certainly, being committed to people's needs and engaging with them firsthand was very fulfilling for me. We did not just visit, we lived in the communities of the people we served. That was a commitment that appealed to me.

Yet I was afraid that if I stayed in the UN, eventually I would lose my own independent mind, the fire in me, and I would be swallowed up by the very organization where I had seen all these bad things happening. I was so afraid that continuing was going to ruin my life. I felt like I was drowning. Maybe I was also losing some orientation in terms of my long-term professional prospects. My mind was straying back to the medical field.

It was at that point that an office colleague, Tim Howick-Smith, told me, "If you stay in the organization, I'm sure you'll be able to influence the organization in time."

Shortly thereafter, there was a recruitment quiz in the UNDP for a career officer. I was sponsored by the Japanese, so if I had really wanted I could go back to Japan to engage in administrative work. So the recruitment quiz was going on. All of a sudden, the time I was about to leave, there was a long telex from the UNDP personnel. I was selected as a candidate to pursue the career track. And among all the junior professional officers, I became the first Japanese to apply at that time.

Then the Resident Representative came to me, and said, "This is the situation. You are recognized as being in the top five percent of all UNDP professional officers. So this is an honor for you."

The Ministry of Foreign Affairs was apparently pleased and phoned the headquarters for my career entry. It slowly dawned on me that I might be a part of Japanese foreign policy for the UN system's support. They needed a way to balance the proportion of Japanese development personnel worldwide with Japan's increasing contribution. To fill in that kind of gap, they already established a certain policy providing for a core, or critical mass of young professionals for the future—and I became part of it.

I was compelled, I was molded in a way. If I decided to forego everything, and went back to Japanese society instead, I risked being ostracized there.

So I stayed, although I was left with questions that I feared I could not answer. And then I got married.

CHAPTER 3

THE COMPANION ARRIVES

Even in the midst of the work, the dangers, discoveries, controversies, and learning experiences in Uganda, I found some precious time for renewing old acquaintances.

Sometime in 1982, Hiroko Satsuma, my friend from the university English Club, wrote to say that she was traveling to Africa by year-end. At that time, I was interested in several ladies whom I was dating. But I took the time to see her. We were together in Nairobi, Kenya, during the Christmas holidays.

She had written once or twice before that to ask for advice. The time I was in the US, it seems, she had been busy working as a teacher aide in an elementary school, and later, with volunteer work in Taiwan.

Her relatives also tried to keep her busy with many "candidates".

She must have met around 30 of them. One in particular, a lawyer, had been serious enough to make her consider marriage. She asked me a few times for my opinion. I was three years her senior at the university, and seemed to her to be someone sensible enough to give advice on life in general.

After our Christmas meetings, things—especially communication—had become worse in Uganda. She offered to take a load of letters and deliver them personally to my parents. My parents were excited that she was coming to visit personally, and besides, she was the only source of news they had regarding my life. She actually stayed a day or two with them, telling them stories, discussing my work, and so on. And through it all, they were struck by her kindness. The youngest of three children, and the only girl in her brood, Hiroko had been the kind of child who never gave her parents any problems, always had good grades, and was often leader in her class.

She had been raised in the city of Osaka. While I got to play in the forest and the river, she played at the lobby of the bank, and strolled around the department store. Also, while her parents had been busy with a prosperous restaurant business, she had grown fairly used to being independent and alone. In a way, that is where she also developed her strength of character.

I had never forgotten that small act of kindness she had done for me at the university. It was the kind of nurturing that she had seen from her mother. The time Hiroko was born—1956—was, in a way, a transition period. Most of the older women in Japan were still truly engaged in the molding of the children and the day-to-day affairs of the household. However, there were already some who were beginning to realize the personal and financial rewards of having a career.

She puts it this way: "It was just get married, become a good helper of the husband—that was the main role for the older generation of women. The younger generation, on the other hand, are focused on careers. I think I'm kind of in the middle. And so I have two feelings: I look up to my mother, and there is something in me that says I have to be a good wife, a good mother but sometimes I feel, well, that's very old-fashioned, and women have to choose their own career."

So she had chosen teaching as a way of having a career. It was flexible enough for her.

At the university, Hiroko had been interested in cultural differences in human relationships. It had been her thesis for her social psychology course. She also liked to read, and was very fascinated with languages. She knew some French and Chinese, and was very fluent in English. Which was why we had been together at the English Club.

What I didn't know was that my father had foreseen that we could be together on a more permanently satisfying basis. A few months after she had been to see them in Japan, my father contacted me by international telephone. At that time, international calls from Japan to Uganda were very rare. It had to be important. It was.

He wanted me to marry her. All I could say was, "Give

me a break. I just need to think." And that was the first time my father lost his temper, telling me, "What I'm trying to do here now is just to marry you off, to stop you from fooling around like this. She's just really a wonderful person. Why not try to get married?" I said maybe, maybe not, and I hung up the phone. I had so many things to consider, not least of which was the new career opportunity and my misgivings about staying in the UN.

I wanted to go back home, partly because I had to look for resources all the time I was in Uganda. A few months later, it turned out that he had signed a marriage document in July 1983, getting me married by "proxy", so UNDP Tokyo sent a telex that went, on such and such a date you married this person. When the telex came my boss jumped. "Shun, are you married or not?!" No, I said. "It says so here. This is the official telex which came from UNDP Tokyo!"

Looking back now, it was a gamble for all of us, especially for Hiroko, considering all the hardships my career had put her through. But my father, it seems, had the clearest vision of us all. He had met her, and known me so well, and perhaps, foreseen that after fifteen years of marriage, I could only have come this far because a person of her character and fortitude was with me every step of the way.

In two short months in 1983 I got married, and signed on for another two years at the UNDP.

I immediately underwent Administrative and Management Training at the UNDP headquarters in New York. I completed the intensive and comprehensive training program that was aimed at raising future senior managers and officials in the UNDP. I was the first selected Japanese trainee to enter that program.

My next posting was waiting, but first I had to prepare Hiroko. I explained to her that the places where I would be going around would be the most difficult countries—and she never thought of that, of how difficult it was. She did not realize at the outset how bad it could be.

In September, 1984, we flew to Ethiopia for a six-month posting. I was assigned to the UNDP office in Addis Ababa as an Administrative/Management Trainee. The field operation was not that long. However, there was conflict going on at that time. There was a series of uprisings against the military rule. There were regional troubles brewing with neighboring Somalia. In the province of Eritrea there were stirrings for independence. To make things worse, the normally hot and mountainous country—where some of the hottest temperatures on Earth have been recorded—was experiencing bouts of serious drought and famine.

After Ethiopia, I was asked to go to the southern part of Sudan, to the city of Juba, one of the last major cities before the Ugandan border. Hiroko was looking at the map but she could see no such city so she asked me, "You are going to Khartoum, you are staying there in the capital, right?" I couldn't say a word. I was afraid she would cry or scream. I just couldn't predict her reaction if I said I was going to cross to the Ugandan border. Once I landed in Khartoum, I just explained where I was going and she was so quiet. She must have kept silent for two days.

In Juba, I worked as an Administrative/ Emergency Operations Officer at the UNDP Sub-office. My main task was to ensure that UNDP's southern Sudan operations for logistics, finance and administration were carried out smoothly. I also had to double as a program officer, and help lay the groundwork for the UN System's future activities in Southern Sudan.

I also served as the regional focal point for emergency operations—"Operation Rainbow"—to rescue displaced people in Southern Sudan, together with representatives of the UNHCR, UNICEF, WFP, donors and other non-government organizations.

These displaced people were mostly refugees from the age-old conflict that had once again ignited between the Christians in the south and the Moslems in the North. We were working mainly in the Christian territory. So the Christian-Moslem fight took place, just like in the Philippines, and I was in the heart of it. We had to close the office.

After that, I thought I was going back to the Headquarters. But I was reassigned to the western part of Sudan in El Fasher, close to the Chad border where another operation of the communists was intense. I had to send my wife back to Japan. The southern part was really falling apart because of the military situation. From southern Sudan I was very close to the Ugandan border. While I was engaged in work in the southern Sudan office there were two coups d'etat that took place in Uganda. I was in touch through radio communications. Some overthrown officials came in to southern Sudan, along with refugees, of course. So the time I was in Africa from 1981 to 1986 there was quite a turmoil; all those countries—Uganda, Sudan, Chad, Ethiopia—were in the midst of troubled times.

And that time we went to Sudan was the only time Hiroko truly realized how difficult things would be.

Our problems were the same everyday.

For her part, she was kept busy with housekeeping because there were no staple food supplies. She always had to boil water for a full 20 minutes, to make sure neither of us got sick. The water for the household came from the faucet; the water from the faucet came directly from the Nile. With insects. Even then, it was scarce. There was electricity in the morning, and sometimes in the evening.

Looking back now, she jokes that her skills in flower arrangement were sadly of no use in Sudan. Had we been in the capital, Khartoum, there may have been a job for her.

At Juba, the market was open only in the morning, from 6:30 to 8:30. Her first concern each day was to look for sugar, salt, and wheat flour—things which were very rarely, if ever, found in the market. There was not even oil for cooking. There was meat, but of poor quality. Fortunately there were some produce like cabbage, and a local vegetable called jili-jili. Fruits were not always available, either. One day there would be pineapples; the next month nothing but oranges. Eggs could be bought—at Khartoum, that is, where there was a flight once a week. Shopping was a very big, serious business for her.

For my part, I was preoccupied with my work, and worried about her at the same time. She often had to get her fish from the Nile. Knowing about the presence of crocodiles there, I thought it was very dangerous for her to be moving around the area. However, she always assured me that she never truly went down into the waters, but merely negotiated with the fishermen who had fish she could buy. Now, whatever things she was able to buy had to be cooked sometimes on a gas stove, but, more often than not (because there was no gas), on charcoal. So it was challenge after challenge for her.

One time the local staff went hunting and came home with a gazelle. Not gazelle meat, but a whole gazelle. She had to join them in the skinning and butchering.

Another time she expressed the desire to eat pork. Most of the people seldom did. One of the staff kindly gave her pork in the form of a whole pig. She was expecting a block of meat, but he brought a pig. She had to clean it herself. Remember this was a city girl who had always thought that meat is from the refrigerator, or the supermarket, and always clean.

Nevertheless, she found out that the lack of options in

Sudan somehow simplified her life. She also managed to cope with the climate soon enough. It was only the security risk that really bothered her.

More significantly, Hiroko was personally involved in fund raising for disabled children. The longer we stayed, the more she became engaged in similar projects to support me. By the time she got out of Sudan, she had become a part of the development work in practice and she could understand it very, very well. I think it helped that she was a teacher, and mature and patient and adaptable. So throughout our stay in Africa, my relationship with Hiroko became really important because we only had each other to rely on. We developed a reassuring, confident and trusting relationship through that hard environment which forced us to rely on each other.

She was not able to join me in El Fasher, though. Located in western Sudan, near the Chad border, we had operations in the middle of the desert. People were dying from widespread famine. I was a group leader (sub-office head) for the emergency operations. There were other NGO's working there.

That was the time that Chad was in the international headlines. This place, although near Chad, was smaller, and it was isolated. There were no roads or infrastructure. By the time we found out that something was happening, it was already too late because hundreds of people were already dying.

The famine was, to some extent, a natural disaster

which had occurred several times before.

Yet there was also the human factor—the civil strife that often affected the flow of food supplies. In some cases during the last couple of decades, Sudan's government tried to cut off food aid to rebels, and the rebels got the civilian's food. Many people were dying because of an artificial shortage of food.

Apart from the human conflict, we also could not communicate easily because of the sandstorms there. When the sandstorms came, everything got buried; people and places got completely cut off. Once, an airplane crashed during takeoff because of a sandstorm.

We were involved in the relief operations for four months straight. Through these, and my involvement with the people, I was trying to find out my weaknesses and strengths; and at the same time discovering the importance of continuing my activities—not anymore for the organization's sake, but for the refinement of my professionalism and personality. I was looking more inwardly at that time, rather than outwardly.

CHAPTER 4

UPHILL FIGHTS

Five years after joining the UN, I fell very ill. I guess it might have been building up in my body, but my physique was somehow overruled by my spirit, by the passion with which I embraced the four straight months of relief work in Sudan.

Right in the middle of the relief operations, a colleague one day casually remarked, "You don't look very well." It was an understatement. I was ill, I had lost weight, I felt weak a lot of times. But I guess the main reason I got sick was the scarcity of water. I was drinking severely contaminated water for some time without even knowing it. I contracted hepatitis, and had to be pulled out of the area to be hospitalized. It was then that Headquarters decided to pull me out permanently.

Upon recovering, I was reassigned to Headquarters, and soon became part of the Division for Audit and Management Review. It was 1986. After chalking up five solid years of field development work, Headquarters had initially thought of assigning me to the Afghanistan operations. But I had to put it off; I really felt my health couldn't make it.

After having been in the bush and the desert for a long time, a cushy management auditor's post at the Headquarters in New York seemed a welcome respite at first. For Hiroko, especially, it was a refreshing change. She was able to learn and teach at Columbia University (eventually, she obtained a Master's Degree for applied Linguistics at the Teachers college, Columbia University) and enjoyed some time with friends. As for me, I had pride in the thought that I was the youngest management auditing personnel in the whole office, only to realize later that I had the most difficult kind of job. On hindsight, nothing in the isolation of a sandstorm-swept desert, or the fear of dying in the jungle, could have approximated the alienation, and the fear of making a wrong judgement, that my new job entailed.

On the surface, the title and work sounded good. I was to be responsible for analyzing UNDP policies and procedures, and advising management of policy implementation issues. Intellectually, very challenging. Physically, comfortable—worlds apart from Uganda, Chad, Sudan. But if Africa wrenched my body, the New York post wrenched my soul.

It was a job that tested my loyalty to the office and to management all the time. I had to audit my previous bosses together with my colleagues. The more I knew, the less I wanted to stay on. After investigating a little more, I caught the syndrome of 1981 once more—I felt I was ready to leave the organization.

I thought to myself, this is an impossible situation: I went back to Headquarters after investing so much time and energy in development work, and risking my life at the front-lines, only to be treated like this, compelled to do something I wasn't prepared for. I didn't want to have any of it much further.

To make things worse, my boss wasn't doing too well, so the directors relied on me a lot, adding to the pressure. In management audit, we were doing basically a police function. Now, if that police function turned out to be just as contaminated as some parts of the system, I had to make a report on that as well. Again, that put me on the spot.

I grew so cynical by the day that I eventually concluded there was only a number of excellent and respectable people working in the organization. I asked myself: "Why do we keep the horrible ones?" I often discussed this matter with my seniors, my colleagues, and sometimes with the few Japanese staff at the Headquarters.

I thought of the UN workers in the field, and the ones who risk their lives as volunteers. They embraced the UN's vision and spirit as their life's mission, yet the perks and the comfortable life were enjoyed by the rotten ones.

Sometimes I even questioned what I did to deserve this

job. In the bluntest sense, I was being turned into a "hit man". And yet I was convinced the rotten ones had to be found out and given their walking papers, and a "hit man" had to help identify them.

I was sucked into a vicious cycle, where the more I did my homework, the better I performed, the more hated I became. Who wants to be promoted for hitting people?

Soon I decided I just didn't fit in that kind of an environment. I preferred the "practitioner" side rather than the "policy" side. I was only 33, and perhaps, I was yearning for some other, more dynamic operation.

One day I mustered enough courage, upped and went to the director: "Could you just release me?"

He replied, "You don't like your work, I know, but I need you and I direct you to stay."

I swallowed hard and said, "Not negotiable, sir."

The director shook his head and soon started negotiating with the Regional Bureau for Asia and the Pacific. Soon my name cropped up for a possible China assignment, as assistant resident representative. Right before that, an option surfaced for me to go to Pakistan.

But I thought hard, and China beckoned. The Tiananmen rallies were taking place, and the democracy movement was abloom. I thought it was an exciting time to go to China. Besides, I had always been fascinated with the place. So the assignment passed to me.

As it turned out many years later when I took a year off and was sponsored by UNDP at the Harvard for a fellowship on international management, perhaps the best pattern for development work is to go through cyclical shifts from practice to theory to practice to theory. That way, each experience enriches the next one.

For all the distaste I had for it later, my New York post somehow complemented, I must concede, the five years I spent in the field in Africa. It became easier for me to spot gaps in policy and implementation because I had seen practice up close.

On the other hand, going back to the field after a stint at Headquarters helps ensure a certain continuity in one's learning process. Thus, six years after field work in Asia (China, then Mongolia), I took the Harvard fellowship and then got posted in the Philippines, where the greatest challenge lay in fostering peace and development in formerly war-torn areas in Mindanao in the south.

It was in the Philippines where I would perhaps combine best the wealth of experience and wisdom from years of study and practice in development work. In the Manila office, I would attempt to combine staff development with field development work. I would eventually come away convinced it was the best approach, under the circumstances.

CHAPTER 5

CHINA OF MY DREAMS

I was assigned in China from June 1989 until 1991, just as relations between the government and the democracy movement took their worst turn ever. I flew in just one week after government troops had opened fire on ralliers at Tiananmen, an episode that represents one of modern China's darkest moments.

Before the massacre, I thought it was a very exciting time to be in a place I had always been fascinated with, and which was then undergoing so many changes. So I let management know I would prefer China to the other option offered, Pakistan.

But one of the weirdest moments I experienced in China was flying in to a virtual ghost town on the first day of my assignment. There were only two of us in the Japan Airlines flight to Beijing, and we had the virtual run of the plane. We were upgraded to first class, treated like royalty by a cabin crew that must have been half-bored with having little to do, and half-mystified by these two people who were going to China at a time of great peril. No one else was going to China because the government had stopped issuing visas to foreigners for a limited period.

I've always thought of China as bustling all times of the day, being the most populous nation on earth. It was weird to see it all quiet when I arrived, with people mortally afraid of talking to foreigners.

Because the shadow of Tiananmen still loomed large, restrictions on both foreigners and native Chinese were stronger than ever. Having been initially billeted in a hotel in the heart of Beijing, I was restless the first night and decided to take a walk at about 7 p.m. I was confident that with my looks, I could easily pass off as a Chinese. Several minutes into my adventure, about 10 soldiers on patrol stopped me and asked if I was a foreigner. I nodded. One asked for identification, informing me casually that there was a curfew at sundown.

"Oh, is that so?" I feigned ignorance.

When one of them saw my ID, he mumbled something apparently having trouble reading English. But the card showed at least where I was staying, and where I was connected, so the soldiers smiled and gave it back to me, advising me to just observe curfew the next time.

I nodded and smiled, but was determined that no one could stop my habit of strolling, especially since I was alone in a strange city. So almost every night I would go out again, trying my best to avoid being spotted by soldiers

CHINA OF MY DREAMS

and singled out as "different". A little later, I started to go with other program officers to the so-called blackmarket, where things normally beyond the reach of ordinary people are sold in stores in between tiny bars frequented by foreigners and students.

I was drawn to the blackmarket because "illegal" things naturally arouse one's curiosity, but also because it proved my point about the Chinese. I've always said the Chinese are the most commerce-oriented people on earth, and that this streak would overcome even the tightest restrictions of a dictatorship. Whether they are in a capitalist or a socialist system, if they can't make the money they need, they would put up some sort of a blackmarket. We were happy to benefit from my theory being proven right.

We spent many an interesting night in those tiny bars—which have no neon signs and no advertising of any sort so as not to attract attention—discussing what was going on and how we might be of relevance. Our discussions were as fulfilling as the service was lousy, however. Many of those who served us were young people, some of them in a hurry to earn extra money in the hope of someday leaving the country. But they were mostly clumsy and naive in their job. The first time I ordered beer, the waiter said he'd check, and then came back with three bottles of beer. I asked why three bottles, and he explained, in halting English and a lot of body language, that he estimated my build to be good for at least three bottles. But I said that even if that were the case, I wouldn't want to be drinking three bottles all at the same time. By the time I finish one, the two others would be warm, I protested. But it was obvious they didn't understand. Or perhaps they were just too lazy to want to come back to a customer's table repeatedly.

A lot of the young staff in those bars loved to watch TV, sometimes glued to the set when CNN was making a report. They waited for and examined advertisements a lot, sometimes ridiculously copying the mannerisms of the models they see in commercials. I remember one Nabisco crackers ad, where the Caucasian model had a peculiar way of handling the biscuits—like throwing cards at a casino table. Before long, the waiters and waitresses were copying that style.

We were not worried about police raids, and I often wondered at the start how these establishments could stay there for long when the whole city was run like a garrison. I got the answer soon enough; the places enjoyed police protection. One would have thought that the authorities secretly tolerated these places so they could easily monitor the movements and eavesdrop on conversations of foreigners and democracy-inclined natives. But the political cause was not even the main rationale for tolerating the bars. Money, it seemed to me then, was the primary reason. The police needed their "cuts," and they were being used to collect money for even higher officials.

Outside the blackmarket area, people tended to be more reticent when approached by foreigners, I found out from Hiroko, who tried to engage some Chinese in conversation at the supermarket or some other public place. That was only in the beginning, though. Midway into our China term, the local people became more vocal in discussing their problems, although they would occasionally look over their shoulders when talking of corruption among cadres, or having to deal with favoritism in the workplace.

Restrictions also reigned in the area where we lived, which was simply called the diplomatic compound. The Chinese were barred from the place, and I remember how one UNDP staffer with a Chinese spouse often encountered problems.

In the office, we faced a situation of extremes, manpower-wise. We had all the best management and program officers, which I found very stimulating and intellectually fulfilling. But the Chinese government restricted us to hiring only Chinese staffers for the rest of the job slots. We virtually had no choice in personnel selection; we had to accept whoever the government sent. These people did not swear by the UN fiat, and we knew that they were also under strict orders to report back to the government what the UNDP was doing. They did so on pain of being sanctioned or ostracized.

Slowly, however, we found a way to make them open up, to make them more trustful of us and, in turn, to be more trustworthy colleagues. Subsequently, we were no longer worried that we were working with spies who did nothing but note down our every little deed or word.

Looking back on all the three years I was there, I must say honestly, however, that the China experience was among the best years of my professional life. I say this with a certain pain, because the people of China went through a crucible with Tiananmen; but the truth is, during China's time of turmoil I really grew so much in my professional life. Part of the reason for this was that most of the UNDP people I worked with in China were top-caliber people. I surmised that all top-caliber people were pooled in China at that time because the stakes were so high.

Hiroko found time to teach in China, too: English composition for Japanese high-school students for one year. She enjoyed the professional community there, as most of the wives of the top-caliber people I worked with were as intellectually stimulating as their spouses.

As Assistant Resident Representative of the UNDP in Beijing, I spent the first half of my three-year term overseeing industrial development policy; the second half in rural development. So I saw the high-technology, most developed regions of China, as well as the most disadvantaged groups and regions. I also saw up close the politics involved in both industrial and rural development policy-making.

I had endless discussions with the Chinese on market socialism, and on how the reforms begun by Deng Xiaoping in 1978 were making an impact on the economy.

I came in as China was on the verge of being pushed

from a time of steady but slow, massive reform in the 80's to one of tremendous, breath-taking changes as Deng demanded a faster pace of his experiment with market reforms in a socialist setting.

His patience was understandable, for it was not only the market reforms that moved slowly. Having closed itself to the world for years, China had suffered technology-wise, and was trying its best to catch up. The Chinese were smart enough to know in their hearts they needed to borrow these from foreigners, but they were even smarter to find ways to use foreign resources for technology improvements without looking like they were so reliant on them.

For instance, they never used the words "aid" or "assistance" to refer to what the foreign development agencies were doing for them. The official term was "mutual collaboration". They apparently loved to use the UN system to get the vital technology that they had missed in the years of isolation. To me, it seemed then that the Chinese had a fascinating way of conducting "industrial espionage." Using the UN system, they were eager to learn something from foreign experts, if only to speed up the pace of modernization required under Deng's blueprint. So, for example, they dealt with the UNIDO (United Nations Industrial Development Organization) a lot. By supporting UNIDO, they were hoping that they could have access to some retired experts or consultants, since direct communication on industrial technology between China and the United

States was forbidden at that time.

The US was cautious about letting communist countries get hold of some strategic technologies and industries. So the Chinese tried to look for other ways to gain access to technology they needed for their economic modernization. One of these avenues was the UN. But the Chinese are very proud people. They never directly admitted that they wanted "aid" in this form, no matter how vital it was to them; and they did not want to be told what they needed. That is why the Chinese were wary of consultants—they hated being told what was wrong in their setup and how these could be remedied.

And because they loathed being told by foreigners what their problems were—it seemed to me that they considered it a strategic weakness to admit—there were instances when problems became full-blown crises. An example: there were no international-level industrial safety standards to speak of. Problems with technology were not openly discussed. One day, there was a big gas explosion in Beijing, later traced to old, less maintained, corroded pipes. I knew from the grapevine that many people died, but it was barely reported in the official media.

I learned later that some prototype pipes that were less prone to corrosion because they were well-coated, were being developed by some foreign experts, but one can almost imagine the kind of cold reception this must have received. So that was our main problem. We were there supposedly to serve, but the people we were supposed to deal with were rather secretive. At the same time, they wanted to know every detail of what we were doing, and scrutinized every imagined motive behind our acts.

Meanwhile, I was painfully aware of the fact that the Chinese regarded their country as a superpower, and that they looked at Japan as a "part" of China. I knew they had a certain difficulty being on the receiving end of any "assistance" from the Japanese, so I kept some distance.

The Chinese are proud of their history, their achievements, their contributions to civilization. They are proud to be a sovereign country, though poor, and at that time it seemed to us outsiders that they are so determined to get what they needed to be ahead that they would squander the one resource they had in abundance—manpower. The Chinese government struck me as one willing to let loose two million people on a major project, despite the risks and the difficult conditions. And, given the political set-up then, I knew the state could get those people there without much protest.

Looking back, it was this political will of the Chinese to carry out what needed to be done to get this big country going, that must partly account for the remarkable growth in the year or so after I came in.

In the early 1990s, China started to enjoy double-digit growth rates, reaching as high as 13 percent annually in 1992 and 1993, a trend unseen anywhere else in the world. That China was such a huge country and economy made the trend even more mind-boggling. Many experts predicted these could not be sustained, painting them as the boom part of a typical boom-bust cycle. Yet they also conceded that the boom-bust cycle aside, the pace of growth was still remarkable, and the most impressive since the 1970s.

One explanation that has been offered for the giddy pace of growth and economic activity in China—at least, before the 1997 crisis struck—credits China's industrial revolution, which has seen real per capita output doubling every 10 years.

I witnessed a great deal of the industrial revolution in my three years in China.

We had identified five areas of concentration for the UNDP in China: human resource development, the technical transformation of existing industries, the development of advanced technologies, the application of electronic information technology and the improvement of living standards.

In the first area—human resource development—we focused on promoting efficiency in advanced science and technology, the effective management of modern enterprises, cutting down wastage of human, material and financial resources.

The second area of concentration—the technical transformation of existing industries—focused on selected existing enterprises in energy, transport, machinery manufacture, electronics, and the chemical, engineering and light industries.

The development of advanced technology was focused on technical hardware and software in the energy sector; the development of new products and the promotion of efficient utilization in various industries; strengthening institutions that provide research and advisory services to industries; and on programs aimed at modernizing industry, promoting increased production, quality control and research and development.

In the application of information technology to meet the needs of end users, project funds were allocated to industry, natural resources, science and technology, general development issues, and agriculture and related areas.

The Country Programme was also concerned with improving living standards in China, especially on matters pertaining to improving diet, income and living conditions.

With the April 1988 midterm review of the Country Programme, a sixth plank was added; economic reform and policy research.

UNDP at that time had invested $20 million in several projects in oil exploration and development, geared toward averting a looming energy shortage. There were six projects in all in the petroleum sector under the Second Country Programme, and among the most important was the Northwest China Bureau of Petroleum Geology's state-of-the-art drilling operations and improvement of drilling proficiency in the Tarim Basin, one of the largest under explored areas in the world. Also important were the petroleum operations project in Nanbao, and the marine engineering geological investigation in the Pearl River-mouth basin of the South China Sea.

The Taklimakan desert in the heart of the Tarim Basin holds one of the most difficult-to-reach oil fields on earth, but also, one of the most promising. The deposits, it has been said, could be three times the US reserves of 74 billion barrels of oil.

Across these potentially rich oil fields, it is said that camel caravans once carried fine silk. This region's role in such a strategic, major trade route has thus made it a veritable melting pot for people and cultures.

The 13th-century explorer Marco Polo, on seeing the oasis cities of Xinjiang in the basin, was said to have exulted: "Everything necessary for human life is here in the greatest plenty...cotton, flax, hemp, grain, wine, and other articles."

If the early explorers looked at Northwest China as a world unto itself, the modern Chinese apparently look to it as a savior of sorts—where energy, something very "necessary for human life," as Marco Polo put it, could be found. Despite the harsh terrain and near-impossible conditions in the Taklimakan, the Chinese officials were determined to explore and maximize its wealth when we came in. Tens of thousands of workers and soldiers would later be sent there, despite the killing temperature extremes and the furious whip of sandstorms, to build an oil road, stretching more than 300 miles, to speed up exploration in desert.

When you have a quarter of the world's people to feed, a possible energy shortage can be so scary that any kind of risk or gamble—even in a hostile desert—could be worth it, I guess.

In all, a total of $128.7 million were programmed under the UNDP's Second Country Programme (1986-1990) for China. The average project size was under $750,000, and a total of 213 projects were implemented. The delivery of projects in 1990 was the highest ever recorded in any country in UNDP history.

In the crafting of the Country Programme, one thing that struck me was how advanced the Chinese were in formulating their own inputs. As far as I knew, they were prepared six to eight months ahead of the UN staff, and then were constantly refined. In fact, the Chinese government had set a two-year timetable for advancing country programs. So by the time we came in, they already knew exactly what they wanted from us.

And by the time we were wrapping up one country programme, they were ready with their country plan for the next five years. They also planned with a long-term view that was both forward and backward, so to speak. They consider what happened in the last 10 or 20 years, how they are faring at present, and then look forward to what needs to be done in the next five years.

And they were very good negotiators. Sometimes one got the feeling they intentionally wore down the other side by endlessly picking on details just so they could get the more substantive concessions.

The main consideration in formulating the Country Programme was its relevance to the five areas of concentration that I cited earlier, which were deemed critical to unlocking the constraints in China's development.

These constraints, as far as we could see, were: the inadequacy of a technological and infrastructure base for rapid development; a weak agricultural sector (worsened by the inadequacy of basic needs of farm communities in some rural areas); a short supply of energy, transportation, telecommunications and raw and semifinished materials; the slow rate of human resource development and skills training to meet the needs of economic reconstruction; the slow improvement of economic performance and technical progress; weak management and administration; and the unsatisfactory rationalization of industrial structures and production mix.

With this view of China in mind, we set about focusing on, first, industrial development and later, rural development. Considering how difficult it is to manage an economy in a country that has one-fourth of the world's population, we were painfully aware of how important it was to maintain a certain balance in pushing it forward a certain direction, especially considering the political turmoil that was engulfing it at that time.

The need for careful management of change is reflected in what has taken place since Deng's call to speed up market reforms in 1992 – after I had left. That call was, as I mentioned earlier, followed by changes that stunned the trained economists in their furious speed and breadth. Double-digit growth rates went with high inflation and wild swings in the stock markets. But I think the Chinese had not foreseen that their building boom would go bust.

Now, some experts say, China is seriously threatened with deflation. Overcapacity and inventories that just keep piling up are the lot of many industries. Foreign direct investment was seen to fall by one-fourth of the previous year's level in 1998. Some critics characterize it as a "bicycle economy" that must pedal ever more furiously just to stay upright.

Again, the instability may be partly rooted in the frenzy of the 1990s, when rural development took the backseat while everyone was blinded by the glitter of a lopsided consumer economy. Many collective farms were abandoned as people who came from generations of farmers suddenly upped and went on to become entrepreneurs.

Many of those who stayed on as farmers now see their farms threatened as more efficient foreign plants edge out their chemical and dairy factories. Worse, state support, a given in all enterprises before the market reforms, is now something they can no longer bank on. The new realities of globalization, liberalization, and privatization have begun to seep in.

As China takes the privatization route and is forced to sell hundreds of bankrupt enterprises, millions of workers have been laid off.

The reforms, using the buzzword of freedom and competition, have brought unbelievable wealth and prosperity for some, but also deepened poverty for others. It's a new ballgame, indeed.

The so-called "freedom" in the market should not, however, be automatically construed as one that translates into real political freedom or greater latitude for human rights. It must not mask the reality that many things still remain to be done to ensure even limited democracy, if there is such a thing.

Come to think of it, I never really appreciated the concept of human rights until I went to China. Every single act seemed bound by certain restrictions, and this must explain why for the most part of my stay there, many locals were reluctant to talk to us – and why many others felt compelled to report on what we, the foreigners, were doing.

Historically, UNDP then was criticized for accommodating too many ideas and subjects without enough resources. It is said that in the end, there was not too much focus on the few areas where it mattered. The UNDP, it seemed, had been compelled to play the role of filling gaps in various sectors between large bilateral banks and bank programmes – and the gaps may not have been effectively filled.

Some gaps were noted when the Third Country Programme was being put in place. It was said that industrial growth must be balanced by a growth in agriculture services and basic infrastructure if the social goals were to be met.

Whatever it was that needed to be done then, or needed to be done now, one thing is clear about China; it remains as one of the biggest challenges to development planners, not just for the sheer size of its area, or population or economy. The complexities of its society are as numbing as its bigness. But I have no regrets about having been part of that attempt to make sense of China's development, especially at a time of profound change.

CHAPTER 6

ROUGH ROAD

All throughout my career, and even during my youth, I had either heard or read, and afterwards, dreamt about going to such places as China and Africa. At no point in my life did I ever think about going to Mongolia.

Yet after I had completed my assignment in China, the opportunity to go to Mongolia came. It was a compelling call to which I could not say so.

Expanse of grassland and desert hemmed in by several mountain ranges, Mongolia shares borders with China and the Soviet Union, the two countries which have understandably had the most impact on the nation's development.

At the outset of this century, Mongolia had declared its independence, but China sought twice to claim it as a province. Since the 1920s, though, it had been Russia that had the most influence on Mongolian government. Mongolia was for the better part of the twentieth century a Soviet satellite, a member of the Council for Mutual Economic Assistance (Comecon or CMEA), the trading bloc of socialist nations. Of all the CMEA member countries, Mongolia was the most dependent on both foreign aid and intra-bloc trade. In fact, 97 percent of the government budget relied on Russia.

Winds of economic change breezed through the country in the 1980s. Government began to relax its controls on production. The more radical changes came by the early nineties. Popular demonstrations prompted a change in leadership, and the newly elected coalition government announced the shift to market economy through a program of privatization and liberalization in trade and economic activities. Unfortunately, the collapse of the Soviet Union and the CMEA trading system came at around the same time. Because of the withdrawal of the Russians, the people started suffering, in terms of education, nutrition, and every other aspect.

True, as with many cases of countries in crisis, an enterprising minority were beginning to earn much higher incomes. On the whole, though, the majority of Mongolians really suffered.

After the Russian withdrawal, almost a fifth of the population slipped below the poverty line. Also, since Russia had previously supplied vegetables and other produce not grown in Mongolia, the majority of the population fell prey to malnutrition. More children were being born underweight and weak. The mortality rate skyrocketed, as did unemployment. Pensioners and single parents were hit really hard.

The government, on the other hand, was simply too beleaguered to respond. It was almost flat broke. Public health and education and other social services had suffered. The public sector also suffered massive loss of human resources, as trained and educated civil servants chose to flee the country.

As if their sudden and total withdrawal was not bad enough, the Russian experts who went away also ripped off everything. Virtually nothing remained. That's how desperate the situation was when the first series of Donor Consultation Meetings were held in 1992. One of the first priorities identified was developing mechanisms to ensure effective aid coordination and management. This came in the form of a comprehensive database on external assistance. The UNDP was tasked with assisting the government in developing the database. Its maintenance and updating was delegated to the Mongolian National Development Board that had been set up during the economic recovery and transition period.

Initial commitments of about $275M were made at a meeting held in Tokyo, co-chaired by the government of Japan and the World Bank. In May 1992, another meeting held in Tokyo provided additional financial support for the remaining part of 1992 and the first part of 1993. Almost $340 million worth of assistance was raised. Most of these came in the form of Balance of Payments (BOP) support and contributions in kind (mainly food and medicine). The UNDP also met with the Mongolian government in Ulaan Baatar to discuss technical assistance.

Through the series of meetings, we were able to identify the most urgent tasks, apart from providing emergency and relief aid. These tasks, which were viewed as medium and long term approaches towards Mongolia's economic transformation, included; the promotion of private sector activity and foreign investment, strengthening of the social safety net, and the rehabilitation and expansion of economic infrastructure.

A Public Sector Investment Program was also drawn up, in which some of the priorities were energy, transport and communications—all key infrastructure sectors requiring donor support; and oil exploration and mineral development, where private foreign sector participation would come in; and urban planning (including water and sewerage) and investment.

In those first two years alone—1991 and 1992—the donor community poured in an average of $300 million a year in assistance, accounting for 15% of Mongolia's GDP during that period. Like what would happen in my work in Mindanao later on, the Mongolian crisis sparked a generous response in the form of over 20 bilateral and 14 multilateral donors.

Hiroko and I flew into the country in July 1992. In years past, the UNDP Resident Representative had always been eastern European or Russian. But the sweeping changes had made Mongolia more open, and politically more free, to accept other nationalities. The government conditioned the people to be open to accept western donors after the so-called Russian withdrawal.

That was a complete policy change for the Mongolian government. At the same time, it was also a complete policy shift in the UNDP to support them. The UNDP had previously avoided placing any of the top caliber people because Mongolia and Russia refused to take any staff from non-communist bloc countries—and ironically, including the Chinese. So there was a personnel policy change. At the same time, allocation of Mongolian resources doubled after they opened up.

So I was part of that change policy of the Mongolian administration. The Resident Representative there was from the Dutch government—Eric De Mul. He was moving back and forth from Beijing because Beijing was a transit country. That time Mr. De Mul and my boss in China, Roy Morey, started negotiating in Beijing. Once it was set up, I couldn't say no. Then again I was pleasantly challenged by the thought of having an almost free hand in changing Mongolia because there was no one there: no World Bank, and very few representatives from bilaterals.

In the face of the daunting task, and in light of the timing of my trips to war-torn Sudan and Uganda, drought-stricken Ethiopia, and post-Tiananmen China, one could say I seemed to be always coming into a place when it was going through its worst time. Of course, I did not design it to be that way. I never planned to go into that. It was just a matter of fact; that's just the way it was.

As Deputy Resident Representative to Mongolia, I was tasked with supervising the preparation and implementation of Mongolia's Country Programme in the transition period. The country program we had drawn up had to be, and was, closely integrated and coherent. It covered broad areas; governance, poverty alleviation and environmental protection.

Not surprisingly, the Resident Representative and myself became the center of everything, the organization would come later. The Resident Representative was extremely dynamic. Unfortunately, though, Eric De Mul, because of his caliber and his performance, was promoted to Mozambique, cutting short his excellent work in Mongolia. Thus, I became acting Resident Representative, until the new Res. Rep. could come. So I was de facto the only UN face, as there was no UNFPA there, and the UNICEF sub-office was very small. There I was, running the office, running almost half the government, running the bilateral program, together with my core staff of about 25 UN personnel, all of them from UNDP. In monetary terms the UNDP had about $25 million in Mongolia at that time.

There was nothing easy or simple about the whole thing. Aid coordination and management was very complex, and became more so as time passed.

Some aid coordination issues arose, which were similar to ones I would later see in Mindanao. These included; insufficient government funds to respond to donors' precondition; a thin (and in Mindanao's case, almost nonexistent) layer of trained professionals to deal with the transitional economy; and inexperience in dealing with international advisors. This last was much more serious in Mindanao, as decades of conflict had entrenched a culture of mistrust among the people.

In Mongolia, there was an initial reluctance to synchronize aid coordination. In some cases this led to an inflexible and compartmentalized way of dealing with aid.

As 1992 drew to a close, nevertheless, it became evident that the government had gained valuable experience in aid management. It became more an issue of how to further improve the government's absorptive capacity as assistance shifted to address Mongolia's long-term structural constraints. The amount of aid Mongolia had received somehow matched the scope of initial work to be done. Therefore, the next important thing was to help train the government human resources and further strengthen their management capacities.

One of the biggest gaps identified was foreign degree

training of senior policy advisors, managers and trainers in market economics and management. Donors pitched in once again in the effort to create a critical mass or core group of market-oriented economists and managers with graduate degrees.

For its part, the government took its role seriously in several areas. One, it had to learn better methods of prioritizing assistance requested. Two, it had to rationalize the roles, procedures, and linkages between and among its various agencies. Lastly, it had to provide a cohesive plan for the most efficient use of technical assistance.

Part of this process was the establishment of the National Development Board (NDB) in mid-1992 followed by the passage of Law on Government, outlining roles and responsibilities of key government units involved in the programming of external assistance. The NDB, being at the helm, was the focus of intense effort, mainly in terms of planning, policy-making and training. Its planning and implementation partners were the Ministry of Trade and Industry, Ministry of Finance, Ministry of External Relations and the Bank of Mongolia.

Apart from training, specific projects were pursued in former or existing State-Owned Enterprises in a wide range of sectors, which included minerals and petroleum, agri-industries, food and garments manufacturing, construction materials, pharmaceutical products and preparations and even the Chinggis Khan Hotel. Additional sectors were later tapped, together with help from foreign suppliers and investors. These included information technologies, dairying, packaging, and even beer brewing, which incidentally, had been one of the very few industries which had fared well even at the height of the crisis.

In those years from 1992 to 1995, Mongolia, with the combined support of the UNDP and the donor community, managed to achieve several things.

First, we had overcome the crisis stage to lay the ground-work for long-term reforms, restructuring and economic transition. Around $20 million had been mobilized by the UNDP alone for the purpose. With the ushering in of information technologies, we had also helped Mongolia overcome its relative isolation from the international community. The Country Programme we had drawn up and implemented afterwards became a model of the Country Cooperation Framework for other Commonwealth of Independent States (CIS) countries. In particular, Mongolia's government reform program was considered as the model case of CIS countries.

By the end of 1993, GDP decline had slowed down. Assistance was shifting to development. And the first two main concerns of the UNDP's program—government reform, and judicial reform—had been addressed quite satisfactorily. The third concern, the change of government (including the electoral system), was addressed as Mongolia had its parliamentary and presidential elections, with a relatively young voter base.

Several sectors were either successfully implementing

reforms, or had been identified as priorities. These included privatization, marketing and irrigation improvements in agriculture and livestock production; improvements in the electric power sector, and the manufacturing sector; the improvement of roads, road freight, urban and air transport, and telecommunications, and sectors like health, education, and the environment.

Nevertheless, we all recognized how critical it was to continue external assistance especially in addressing Mongolia's severe social problems.

By the time most of the reforms were underway, however, I could already appreciate deeply the kind of work that had been required and done in Mongolia. It had all been a sort of "explosive" stage for me; all my accumulated knowledge and experience had been tested and greatly enriched in Mongolia. This could be the last stage in my career, I thought then. At that point what I really wanted to do was to obtain more knowledge and make myself more marketable in the UN and any other organization, so I could do anything I wanted.

From the start, it had been my professional ambition to influence the government to change. It was the greatest achievement I could think of. And it happened.

Tragically, in the process of achieving all these, I had neglected something inestimably significant; my relationship with, and the happiness of my wife, Hiroko.

As I was busy with my work, she had chosen to take advantage of her teaching background. She was involved with the university in Mongolia and the national radio station. In the latter she taught Japanese. I was confident that she had her own preoccupation. She never complained, so I thought everything was all right but it was not.

She had her own equally daunting challenges, too. I was to find out later.

Among these was the weather condition. The winters in Mongolia are punishing, to say the least, at a typical minus 40 degrees. The winters are dark, and must have contributed to her overall sense of isolation.

As Hiroko describes it now: "Suddenly it was almost beyond my capacity. I think I almost had a nervous breakdown. In Mongolia, I didn't have a good UN community, or a good support group."

The deeper, greater difficulty lay in the fact that she had not really been able to bond with any one of the UN staff or their wives. There had been less than 20 Japanese women she could possibly associate with. All throughout our stay there, there had only been one Japanese lady, the wife of a Japanese businessman, who had become close with Hiroko. Sadly, the traditionally hierarchical sense of Japanese relations had been somehow transplanted to our small community in Mongolia, and relationships among the women were limited and defined by their husbands' respective standings. Other embassy staff wives somehow shied away from Hiroko, as they were conscious that she was near the top of the UN group. It was compounded by the fact that she was one of the few English-speaking

Japanese around. This added another element of isolation, as non-English-speaking Japanese did not initiate communication with the English-speaking ladies.

Outside of that circle, Hiroko could not really confide to friends based in Japan, as she sensed that somehow, the uniqueness of her experiences had given her a distinctly different perspective that her old friends might not be able to relate to.

Prior to our arrival in Mongolia, she had actually already been suffering from frustration and fatigue, and the pressure not to have a child, and the strains and stresses of having to keep moving around the world, and feeling disoriented. By the time we had reached Mongolia, her frustration had reached the peak.

One day it just exploded. She wanted to divorce me.

She did not say it in so many words, but she said she needed to cool off. That really hurt me. And it came at the time I was engaged in the middle of the government's economic reform, and living through the most important, the most difficult yet most rewarding time for me, when work was going well. The UNDP had become the center of the world for me.

Initially, I thought she was actually fine and had simply begun to want to do something else. It was not a physical disease, which may have been easier for me to grasp instantly. Slowly, however, she helped me understand that she was really mentally sick, exhausted, and simply couldn't work any longer.

With her perceptiveness and intelligence, she knew fully well I was absorbed in my job, and she understood that I wanted to go further. Torn between that and her own feelings of being unable to go on, she was telling me, "I'm sorry, I know you want to go higher, but I don't want to go on anymore. However, I'm not stopping you."

It wasn't a case of her wanting to leave and try something different; it was nothing like that at all. Throughout the difficulties we had experienced in Africa, she had managed to cope somehow because she took pride in herself, and knew what she could do. She was not one to quit easily. But even then, she felt that our life was very tough, and she slowly began feeling unsure about her ability to cope. She knew the kind of person I was by the time we had gotten married. She appreciated fully well the significance of what I wanted to do.

Pragmatically, she said to herself, "This is the husband I chose...I knew this. Now, maybe I have to leave him, because I can no longer fulfill my role in the kind of partnership we have. I have tried my best. But I cannot handle it anymore. I must choose to leave."

It had become a matter of survival for her.

What made it tough was the time element. In the beginning, she had psyched herself up believing that Mongolia would be a two-year posting, after which we would be moving to Harvard. For two years, as she later described it to me, "I really braced myself, knowing that though these two years would be hard, after that I'd go to Harvard."

One year and a half later, though, I had told her, we'll stay one more year.

In her own words; the announcement "really knocked me down."

Hiroko explains how it felt.

"It's like a marathon run. You've walked 30 kilometers and you're thinking, it's just ten kilometers more, then somebody tells you, you've got to run more. If from the beginning I'd been told I'd have to run 50 kilometers, maybe I would have planned myself that way. But what happened was very different. Having to prepare for one more year, after two years—that was very hard."

As for me, her disclosure made me stop looking at my career. For me, things had become simple and clear. I didn't want to lose my wife. That was my top priority and I just forgot about everything else.

I told her that we had to give ourselves a chance again. After all, we'd held together for 12 years all in all, and we were not going to just throw everything away. I just asked her to give us a chance and I was going to take one year off.

If it still didn't work then we would decide. It was a major turning point in our lives. She wanted us to go back to Japan and leave the UNDP, and just start all over again. I thought that was a very important choice to consider. Finally, we took one year off; I went on a sabbatical to Harvard.

But even that move was controversial because some

people said that in doing that, I was going to delay my career, and I was going to be eased out. Others said it was an excellent move; and that type of move was needed to refresh and "retool" me, and renew my interest in UNDP policy.

When I look at the whole thing now, I realize how difficult it really is to balance commitment to development work, and commitment to family; but I also see that it is well worth the immense effort required.

Hiroko and I have both changed much, though subtly, in the course of our marriage and my work. As a young girl, she had always seen herself to be outgoing in comparison to her peers. These days she feels more of an introvert. The quiet moments she has with me and our son Keiichiro are part of her "recharging" perhaps, a means to cope with the heavy social demands of having a husband like myself, one who, by choice and necessity, often has to entertain and mingle with people. There is also the fact that she has to adjust to entire cultures for stretches of time, and subjugate her own desires and tastes to the demands of the cultural setting we find ourselves in. Her innate sense of balance is often tested to the limit.

All these realizations have taught me to be more sensitive to Hiroko's behavior. I had always known how strong and active she can be. But now I could see also how vulnerable she could become as I pursued my own work.

It was clear we needed time together as a family, far away from the very involved nature of field work that I had been doing in all sorts of strange lands. So we took that much needed break in 1995. It was actually to become a most rewarding break in all aspects.

For one, it was during our stay in the United States that Hiroko was able to conceive our son, Kei. The more relaxed atmosphere must have helped immensely. Also, it has been in the United States where Hiroko has, in the past, been able to "retool" her own sense of self. For instance, it was during our time in Harvard where she met a Japanese artist who taught her pottery. She had fulfilling moments learning to make pottery, and honed her strong sense of form and shape.

Interestingly, her sense of aesthetics seems to give a glimpse of her character. She does not consider herself as having a good sense of color. She prefers to focus on form, and likes pottery in black and white—stark, striking, defined.

Our relationship was healed and strengthened as we spent a lot more time together, talking, sorting things out. We were able to understand better some of the things we had gone through.

It was also the perfect time to assess both my direction and that of the UNDP. I belonged to the Harvard Institute of International Development as a visiting researcher. I entered a mid-career program sponsored by the UNDP, under which I later completed my Master's degree in Public Administration (majoring in Strategic Management) at Harvard University's Kennedy School of Government in

1996.

It was truly a fortuitous time. The time we were there, mid-career people from all over the world were there. It was rejuvenating and refreshing to see not just myself in development work, but also public sector professionals from different countries.

At the same time, I had the luxury of being able to ponder on the strengths and shortcomings of my organization.

Some of the most important products of that reflection were two comprehensive papers that I submitted for my subject in Organizational Culture: Managing Public Sector Change, and in Strategic Human Resource Management. They both dwelt on the "UNDP in Transition: Crisis or Opportunity?"

The more I reflected deeply on the UNDP's problems, its strengths and weaknesses, and the challenges it faces, the more I realized that sometimes—as in my personal life, where something near-tragic jolted me—crisis creates an opportunity for being and doing better. Provided, however, one does not flinch in front of the mirror, and calmly assesses the damage from the storm.

With as clinical an attitude as possible, I plunged headlong into studying the organization I had worked for four years, wanting to see where both it, and I, were best headed.

The UNDP is the world's largest multilateral source of grant funding for development cooperation. It was created in 1965 through a merger of two predecessor programs for UN technical cooperation. Funds come from the voluntary contributions of member states of the UN and its affiliate agencies, providing roughly US$1 billion yearly to UNDP's central resources.

A 36-member Executive Board composed of both developed and developing countries approves major development programs and policies for developing countries. Through a network of 132 offices worldwide, UNDP works with 174 governments to build developing countries' capacities for sustainable human development; poverty elimination, environmental regeneration, job creation, and the advancement of women. The UNDP is in a unique position within the UN System to evaluate and coordinate the many UN and other multilateral and bilateral aid activities carried on in the development world. The system is decentralized to give substantial authority to the head of the UNDP (the UNDP Resident Representative, who doubles as the UN Resident Coordinator in a country), and this is reflected in the deployment of staff resources (850 professionals and 3,000 general service staff). In UNDP headquarters, there are only 150 professionals and 500 general service staff; and in the UNDP country office, 700 professionals and 2,500 national staff.

The UNDP'S avowed mission is primarily to help the UN become a powerful and cohesive force for sustainable human development; strengthen international cooperation for sustainable human development, and serve as a major substantive resource on how to achieve it—mainly functioning as a development service provider.

In the course of my studies, I had raised several points which I saw, during that time, as crucial to improving the UNDP's donor relations, internal communication and efficiency, as well as service delivery capacity. Among the specific factors I raised, many of which have since been partly or fully realized and addressed, were:

- Efficient staff resources utilization and mobilization, where UNDP staff, not just the management, participate actively in donor relations. It could go as far as having UNDP staff (who are from developing countries) help and advise the UNDP country office as an effective liaison with the aid recipient governments to advocate the UNDP performance.
- An institutionalized staff exchange program between the aid recipient governments, the donor governments and the UNDP staff (the staff will be a catalyst and facilitator for aid policies and implementation between the organizations.)
- A mandate for the UNDP country Resident Representative to communicate donor relations with the HQ as well as with other country offices in the region. The learning experience must be shared in terms of donor participation in the development project cycle.
- A "Donors' Profile" (an analysis of donors' agenda, whom to be contacted, who was contacted previously,

what was the outcome, why it failed or why it succeeded, etc.). The data base has actually been created, containing the relevant individual report, management report and country report; eventually, all these will be accessible to all UNDP staff through E-mail.

Finally, since we are heavy on capacity building and human resource development, the organization should take the lead in encouraging freer flows of communication among its staff, regardless of hierarchies. I advocated then an E-mail Forum where staff could freely exchange notes or sound off each other on issues that some of them may be reluctant to bring up with management. I believed then—and I still do—that free discussion of substantive issues is the best medium for bringing to the fore as well the personal dynamics among people in the organization. In discussing, for instance, how a poverty reduction program should be carried out, the staff are inevitably drawn into discussing as well the personnel requirements of such an undertaking. Then, people who would normally be reluctant to talk about personal approaches and job delineations per se would have an outlet for discussing these matters, using the substantive part of the projects as springboard.

This very same approach would, several months later, serve me in good stead, as I jumped from my pit stop to an entirely new landscape, the Philippines. By combining human resource development of the staff with project management, we ended up with a situation where development practice virtually shaped the theories, rather than the theories making the development practitioners. People who make the theories or espouse them should practice first—I have always advocated that. And our experience in Mindanao proved to be infinitely enlightening to all of us in UNDP Manila.

Sometime during our stay in Harvard, I found myself considering not going back to the UNDP. The recruitment staff in Harvard asked me to undergo some interviews with other organizations. I had just one interview with a multinational bank.

It all seemed worth considering, until they posed one condition: I had to travel every six months. So it was the same problem all over again. Hiroko would again always be wondering where I was—whether I was in Tokyo or in Mongolia. And I would be in one place half of the year, and in another the next six months. It was the same dilemma, and at last I felt I didn't need to consult my wife because I knew she would say no. I finally refused them.

Then in 1995, I got a telephone call from the UNDP Regional Bureau for Asia and Pacific. I had come down to headquarters for an interview. I already knew what was happening: I was going to stay on the Asian bureau.

The first thing the deputy bureau director at that time told me was, "Shun, you're going to either Pakistan or the Philippines. You don't seem to have many choices. But this is something I already discussed with the bureau director.

The Philippines may be providential, but as an option just think about Pakistan."

I didn't know what was happening in the Philippines. But as I was to find out later, they had given me a good option. The Resident Representative during my Philippine posting, Ms. Sarah Timpson, and I had a certain complementariness in our work experiences.

I talked with Hiroko about it. She consented to giving it a try, considering that both of us perceived the Philippines as being relatively safe. So I finally prepared myself, Hiroko, and my young son, Keiichiro, for our new tropical post.

CHAPTER 7

A NEW LANDSCAPE AWAITS

Mindanao. The very name breathes challenge and inspires awe in an outsider. The second largest island of the Philippines, home to 15 million people, a third of them Muslims, Mindanao has been the waterloo of many an outsider since the time of the Spanish conquistadores.

For centuries, the people of this ethnically and culturally diverse region have taken pride in being consistent fighters of any alien invasion. hey have scoffed at the Spanish, American and Japanese invaders, pledging to do battle anytime so as to be left alone in peace.

Yet ironically, the one kind of outsider they would fight most bitterly after the foreign invaders leave would be their own Filipino blood brothers. Because of its vast area, rich natural resources (minerals, some of the country's last major virgin forests, energy sources like big bodies of water), and big pockets of relatively unexplored and little-inhabited territory, Mindanao had been treated like a haven of sorts for decades by settlers from Luzon and the Visayas. Little wonder that a good number of the people of Mindanao speak a Visayan dialect.

Most of these settlers are Christians, and so, for as long as one could remember, the subsequent conflicts, mostly economic, that erupted between settlers and original inhabitants increasingly became characterized as a religious war, with both sides ascribing to each other's faiths the defects that should be more logically attributed to cultural practices and lifestyles and norms, or even to individual follies.

Thus did the Muslim poor for decades blame the "greedy Christian landowners" for taking their land and resources. In turn, the Christians would fall into the trap of calling the criminals "Muslim bandits." Yet Christianity never sanctioned greed in the same way that the Koran never tolerated banditry.

To be sure, the foreigners never really left the place, staying on at least as benign (read; just here to do business) visitors and not as overt occupiers. They were alternately blamed with the Filipino settlers for exploiting solely for their own benefit—it was perceived—the vast resources of Mindanao. In the early 70's, the Muslim rebellion was met with the full military might of the Marcos regime. The military has its hands full fighting, not only the Muslims who demanded secession under the banner of the Moro National Liberation Front (MNLF), but also the communists and their military arm, the New People's

Army. The communist rebels found fertile ground for proselytizing because Mindanao, for all its wealth, manifested the most tragic discrepancies in wealth and was home to millions of marginalized ethnic groups.

Davao City and the Davao provinces, especially, became virtual "laboratories" for the communists, who fielded the dreaded "Sparrow" hit squads against those whom they considered abusive landlords, soldiers, policemen, politicians and criminals.

Ironically, the conflict would fuel the very same misery that it was rooted in. As endless war—between government and Muslim rebels and government and communist rebels—took its toll, new investments eventually were discouraged and some of the old ones took flight with every new wave of peace and order breakdown. Public infrastructure was at a standstill in many places, with schoolhouses closed down by the fighting, and children idled by the closure of their schools were left with two choices—in truth, virtual nonchoices—to either work the fields or join the rebel army.

Poverty became an unstinting reality. Thus, just before the Philippine government and the MNLF forged their historic peace agreement on September 2, 1996, the face of Mindanao was simply one of unmitigated poverty. Fourteen of the 20 poorest provinces in the Philippines are from Mindanao. Twelve of these 14 are within the Special Zone of Peace and Development (SZOPAD), with a poverty incidence of 51.2 percent as of 1991 and 1994.

The disaggregated Human Development Index (HDI)—a measure of the human development of a place that combines achievements in longevity rates, income and education—cited in the 1997 Philippine Human Development Report showed alarming disparities between the quality of life in Mindanao and in Metro Manila, which was at the top of regions with an HDI value of 0.871.

In contrast, Western Mindanao lay at the bottom, with an HDI value of only 0.410. If our regions were compared to countries, Western Mindanao would be next only to Zambia, which ranked 143rd in the world HDI tables, versus the Philippines' rank of 98th.

This was the Mindanao that needed to be "saved" in many different ways, as the promise of peace finally dawned in September 1996.

The irony of life in Mindanao was so stark it could make one cry. How, one wonders, could so many people wallow in misery amid such bountiful resources? How could time stand still for people trapped in decades of war while the rest of the world—including similarly strife-torn places—marched on in progress?

The Mindanao peace agreement was signed in September 1996, just two months after I got my posting as deputy resident representative to the Philippines. Because of my background in Africa and Mongolia, my first instinct was that I wanted to do something to help jumpstart the post-conflict rehabilitation there. But the big events in Mindanao caught me in the midst of serious, backbreaking work as I attempted, foolishly at first perhaps, to make sense of what I thought then was a failure to maximize the rich store of human resources at the UNDP's country office in Manila.

I was in the middle of trying to reinvent the office, so to speak, trying to prod the staff to turn it around as a truly development-oriented agency, not a research office.

To be sure, the people in the Manila office were good planners. They were producing beautiful project documents. The UNDP staff in Manila certainly had tremendous potential. But something seemed to be missing, a critical element that I initially could not put a finger on. People seemed to be good at working on their own, but not so much as a team. It looked like that at the time.

So for at least one month, I took time out to talk to each member of the staff, from the highest-ranking programme officer to the administration people, even the messengers and drivers. I spoke to them individually, asked them about their ideas of the UNDP's—and for that matter, the UN's —role, and what they hoped to contribute. I asked them their problems, and I was pleasantly surprised by the candor in which they gave their answers. I wrote down their answers in capsules, in differently colored slips of paper, which I still keep to inspire me.

Having thus known the staff's expectations, both professional and personal, I could chart, with greater confidence, my own map of how to go about making this office a lean and mean one, something relevant to the great challenges that lay ahead.

The message soon went around, I guess, that I was serious about this side of my work. Soon, I changed the pattern of organizing work, making it more group-oriented, with more group decisions. And the delegation of work was really followed.

The UNDP's internal problems were compounded then by what I thought were rather weak links between and among the UN agencies.

Suddenly, suddenly, Mindanao beckoned. Why not, I thought, do both at the same time? Go to Mindanao, bring the UNDP and the UN agencies and the donors to Mindanao and make them work with the people, and at the same time turn the UNDP staff into a fighting, working machine? In other worlds, I was meaning to combine project management with human resource management.

It seemed a highly complicated challenge, one that would require a lot of balancing in terms of resources, time, effort, and, most important, the dynamics of human relationships, as people who were not used to working together would suddenly be forced to do something very challenging, and very new, together.

But then I thought a chance like this could never happen again. Besides, having taken pride in my work in Africa and Mongolia, I decided that I would be a coward not to take on this challenge. If the people of Mindanao desired peace enough to take the risky path of a settlement, then they deserved, as well, to have a better life.

They needed to be vindicated in their decision to take the extra mile for peace. And the UN, I thought to myself, must help them attain such vindication.

Over the past two and a half years that we have been involved in the southern Philippines, I've found that there are many parallels between my work in Africa and, 15 years later, in Mindanao. In a sense, Africa prepared me well—though the experience was not exactly the same—for the challenges of Mindanao.

In Uganda, as I said in Chapter 2, my first job was to mingle with the community of the Karamojons, a group of people with a strategic role of stabilizing Uganda politically. They're armed and fierce warriors—much like the Moro rebels of Mindanao.

And like the Karamojons, who take time to trust but really support you once you've earned their trust, the people of Mindanao behaved similarly.

There are parallels as well in the physical environment. Food was hard to find and one had to bear with primitive facilities. There were no stable sources of clean water, no electricity, very little of health care systems. There were, though, rough roads that one must sometimes traverse on foot for hours.

But the real test in both places was this—that you never give the people a reason to doubt your sincerity to help, your determination not to make the situation any worse than it already is. As in Uganda, we used a mix of emergency food supplies and basic materials and tools for livelihood, like plows, seeds and carabaos, at the start, to demonstrate such sincerity.

The first two months were really the test, a bonding, confidence-building experience. It required a lot of patience, and especially an understanding of the cultural nuances and dynamics of the situation.

Yet another similarity between my Ugandan and Mindanao experiences was the presence of a multinational development assistance community in both cases. After my work with the Karamojons, I was involved in the rehabilitation of Uganda, which was damaged in the protracted struggle between Idi Amin and Milton Obote. I was assigned to rehabilitate first, Lake Victoria and second—the most challenging actually—Entebbe. UNDP was in charge of the Entebbe airport rehabilitation, but Americans, British, the Dutch, and other nationalities from Europe were represented in that undertaking. Same with Mindanao, where, as soon as the UN System jump-started the delivery of services to former MNLF communities, we got 11 countries (Australia, Netherlands, New Zealand, Spain, Canada, Switzerland, Sweden, Norway, Belgium, Japan, Germany), the European Union and three multilateral organizations (ADB, World Bank, USAID)) to join our multi- and bi-cooperation programs.

My experience in the other African assignments—Ethiopia, then Southern Sudan—also mirrored the kind of risks that I would later encounter in Mindanao. All that time I was in Africa—from 1981 to 1986, there was turmoil. The southern part of Sudan, Juba, saw some very fierce fighting between Christians and Muslims.

My wife and I were there for two years. We were in Christian territory, but the northern part of the place was Muslim-dominated.

Afterwards, I was reassigned to the western part of Sudan, near the Chad border, where there was also turmoil. Also, in Africa as in Mindanao, famine compounded the civil strife.

Another complication in both places; the state of preparedness of the aid recipients. In Africa we were moved into weighing if we were asking the recipient countries too much. We had the same misgivings in Mindanao.

The former MNLF communities in Mindanao had been at war for a quarter of a century at least. They had known no other job than to fight for what they believed was right—political freedom, and more important, an end to economic exploitation and marginalization; they had known no other occupation than to be a soldier. They were, in the UNDP-Philippine team's words, inured to a "culture of taking orders" from commanders, not to a culture of taking initiatives.

It shouldn't have been surprising that it was difficult to get them to handle the aid, divorced of all their cultural norms and standards. In their communities, for instance, people did things on the basis of whom they know, and so it was hard at first to get them to understand why we needed to have formal biddings for rice and other emergency foodstuff—they ask why they cannot just buy them from people they knew? Moreover, when we started recruiting people to man the local field teams—as part of the job generation part of the program, we hired MNLF community members to conduct the group discussions, field questionnaires, etc.—they asked why we needed to set such neutral qualifications or requirements which sometimes tended to shut out the very people they knew, as they could not qualify.

Even the MNLF leaders apparently realized the trickiness of handling material resources when people have very high expectations about being able to quickly attain the promise of a better life that they envisioned with peace. At the April 14-15, 1997 workshop in Cotabato City, it was decided—after the MNLF made the request—that all forms of assistance delivered as part of the post-conflict projects should be in kind, not cash. Emergency aid would be in the form of food, mainly rice and supplements like sugar, canned goods, coffee, and medicine. Livelihood assistance, too, would be in kind.

Several factors influenced the MNLF decision to seek non-cash assistance, according to the Terminal Report. "One, unfamiliarity with handling donor cash. Second, cash assistance would create more problems; jealousies, intrigues and false accusations among various interest groups within the MNLF. Third, the MNLF leaders thought that handling assistance in kind would allow them to learn by doing without the added complication that accounting for cash would entail."

After weeks and weeks of immersion in the area, of endless exploratory sessions and meetings, we finally started to realize that sometimes, the peace process requires compromising, if only to build confidence. We set the rule that whenever and wherever possible, we would try to accommodate their suggestions and wishes—but always, without jeopardizing some very basic standards for rendering assistance. We had to impress on them that confidence-building works both ways, that they also have to grant some concessions, make some sacrifices and change some ways.

The give-and-take was lengthy and arduous and complicated. But as our technical staff's Final Report in 1998 put it, it was all worth the struggle.

The UN's direct involvement in the Mindanao peace process began a few weeks after the signing of the peace agreement in September, 1996. The National Economic and Development Authority (NEDA) requested the UN's assistance in conducting a needs assessment and capabilities survey among MNLF combatants, their families and communities. Soon after that, the Philippine government formally sought the UN's assistance in peace and development work.

Between the signing of the peace agreement and the end of the first quarter of 1997, we got deeply involved in—in fact, initiated for the most part—a series of meetings among stakeholders to define priority activities for confidence-building and long-term development.

Within a three-year period, the peace agreement had defined a two-phased implementation and mechanism. The immediate tasks were covered in Executive Order 301 signed on October 2, 1996, by then President Fidel V. Ramos, proclaiming the Special Zone of Peace and Development (SZOPAD) and the Consultative Assembly. It also mandated the integration of 5,750 MNLF members into the Armed Forces of the Philippines and of 1,750 more into the Philippine National Police.

(The area of autonomy agreed upon in the Tripoli Agreement covered the provinces of Basilan, Sulu, Tawi-Tawi, Zamboanga del Sur, Zamboanga del Norte, North Cotabato, Maguindanao, Sultan Kudarat, Lanao del Norte, Lanao del Sur, South Cotabato, Palawan and all cities and villages in these areas. The same area, including the new province of Sarangani, which was carved out of South Cotabato, now constitutes the SZOPAD.)

For the ex-MNLF combatants who could not be absorbed into either the police or military, the document mandated a "special socioeconomic, cultural and education program...to prepare them and their families for productive endeavors, provide for educational, technical skills and livelihood training and give them priority for hiring in development projects."

Another memorandum, signed a day earlier on October 1, 1996, directed 21 Philippine government agencies to formulate "an overall framework" for precisely such a program for the displaced MNLF combatants. That interagency Special Development Planning Task Group was headed by the NEDA. The agencies agreed on an initial strategy; find out first what exactly these people needed and wanted. Services would then be provided through three entry points; direct to the MNLF individual and/or family; through community organizations (e.g., cooperatives, village associations); and through institutions/organizations, including local government units.

The Terminal Report recalls how later, from consultations of the interagency group with the MNLF state chairman, four categories of social projects were identified as priority needs; education, training and social services; livelihood and employment; land ownership, distribution and production; and infrastructure and utilities. The government then created the Interagency Technical Working Group (IA-TWG) for the Formulation of a Framework and Package of Programs and Projects for MNLF Elements Not Absorbed by the Military.

The immersion that I talked about earlier took place between October and December of 1996. Nur Misuari, who had by then been elected governor of the Autonomous Region of Muslim Mindanao (ARMM), in a meeting with UN agency heads, asked the UN System to get involved in the SZOPAD, particularly by leading in relief operations with the Southern Philippines Council for Peace and Development (SPCPD). Subsequently, Sarah Timpson, the UN Resident Coordinator in the Philippines, met with Muslimin Sema, the SPCPD's executive director, regarding arrangements for the emergency assistance.

The involvement in the needs assessment work was finally cemented at the first meeting of the SPCPD's Consultative Assembly in General Santos City on February 18–19, 1997, when such an agreement was reached with representatives of UNDP and UNICEF. I quote from the Terminal Report: "The programme directly involved the MNLF provincial commanders in an assessment of needs and of existing capabilities, on which a new programme could be built. MNLF freedom fighters, who before the war were schooled in academic institutions, were being tapped for their skills in, for example, providing health services or organizing livelihood programmes. The goal was to ensure that MNLF leaders had a hands-on exercise in the tools of development—in focused group discussions and consultations, survey instruments, cooperatives and community organizing. The programme was placed under the overall supervision of the SPCPD."

As of February 1998, the SPCPD-UN-NEDA-Multidonor programme was carrying out 24 projects benefiting 1,627 families of former combatants in 30 towns covered by six MNLF states.

The needs assessment survey was done on a pilot basis in six MNLF states only: Lumatil in Maasim, Sarangani; Salbu in Datu Piang, Maguindanao; Madalum in Lanao del Sur; Tictapul in Zamboanga City; Indanan in Sulu; and

Puerto Princesa in Palawan. Sixty respondents in each pilot area (or 20 percent of the total number of beneficiaries) were interviewed. Two key instruments were used—the main survey itself using a seven-page interview, complemented by focused group discussions.

Field cluster teams were trained in late April 1997 to do the interviews; and after this training, a field survey was immediately begun alongside an information drive. Alongside the needs assessment survey, food assistance and livelihood projects were outlined and prepared.

The delivery of food assistance, though slightly delayed, was given priority because it was seen as critical to stemming the tide of restlessness that quickly—and understandably—enveloped former combatant communities who were eager to see quick results. It was hard telling people that the dividends of peace take a long time coming, when all they worry about is feeding their families.

The needs assessment survey was completed in four months, after numerous and unavoidable interruptions.

Afterwards, a decision was made to expand the coverage to 10 areas, and further emergency assistance was provided. From emergency assistance, preparations were made to go into long-term planning for livelihood programs. After all, the main objective of our intervention was to help the tens of thousands of former combatants who would not be integrated into the military or the police force.

UNDP assisted in cooperative formation and community organizing for livelihood, providing about 12 million Peso to some 12,258 MNLF beneficiaries. This package of assistance is in addition to the assistance in the first phase covering six pilot areas and about 1,800 individuals and their families.

Agro-based livelihood training assisted by FAO in the areas of aquaculture, crops, farm machinery, livestock, women concerns, among others, covered almost 2,000 trainees with a total cost of 11.7 million Peso.

The trainings resulted in the establishments of 532 livelihood projects in 158 MNLF communities. Examples of these were vegetable seed and planting materials, solar driers and fish cage production. These projects benefited some 20,084 MNLF combatants and their families.

As I was writing this chapter, many new developments started to surface in Mindanao again. Since the first edition was released, the Estrada administration first, and then the government of President Gloria Macapagal-Arroyo, had to deal with a resurgence of rebellion and lawlessness involving several groups.

Sustaining peace and development in the South has thus become problematic.

In March 2000, then President Joseph Estrada declared an all-out war policy, resulting in heavy fighting until rebel camps were overrun.

The following month, at Easter, a loose band of armed men who claimed to be Islamic "fundamentalists" and calling themselves the Abu Sayyaf Group abducted a group of foreigners from a Malaysian resort and slipped them into the southern Philippine islands of Basilan and Sulu. The hostage scandal focused international media attention on Mindanao at a time when the south was just being projected as a showcase in development efforts of government owing to its agricultural potentials and largely untapped areas.

The peace process again was put on trial, with the military launching prolonged military operations in several provinces, particularly in Central and Western Mindanao. The Department of Social Welfare and Development reported a total of 68,381 families were directly affected by the armed conflict in the SZOPAD areas.

Three months later, the Estrada administration declared victory over the MNLF whose main camp in Maguindanao, Abubakar, was overrun.

In an effort to regain investors' confidence in the south, Mr. Estrada also signed Executive Order No. 262, constituting the Mindanao Coordinating Council (MCC), which he himself chaired. The council was supposed to "act as the overall coordinating body to ensure the integration, synchronization and accelerated implementation of plans, programs and projects to rehabilitate Mindanao, specifically in the areas affected by the conflict."

This latest direction, in terms of government's recognition of Mindanao as a priority area for rehabilitation efforts and development in the context of the conflict situation, presented an invigorating opportunity for the

UN/MDP in its third phase. This strong government stance, supported by the GOP's poverty eradication program, guided the successor phase in its efforts to preserve the gains of the 1996 peace pact agreement, the UN later noted.

The second phase largely covered provisions for political representation and transition for the MNLF within the framework of the Philippine Constitution and its laws. The next phase built on the fact-finding, needs assessment and community action planning and pilot emergency assistance implemented under the first phase of the program.

The 1996 peace agreement provided for a three-year transitional period that technically ended in September 1999, followed by the establishment of a new autonomous government to be determined by a plebiscite. The transition period was briefly extended through an executive order. .

While there were serious efforts on both sides— the government and the MNLF leaders—to sustain the gains from the peace process, the Estrada administration collapsed, and the emergence of a new government under Gloria Macapagal-Arroyo brought new policies, particularly in the peace and development efforts.

Finally on August 14, 2001, a plebiscite was conducted, putting in place a new organic act. The island province of Basilan and Marawi—which has the distinction of being the only Islamic city in the country—were included in the ARMM, which had originally covered only four provinces.

The change in government policy, however, has not affected the UN-led program's priority and focus, not only because it had already made inroads in institutionalizing direct peace and development interventions. The SZOPAD area remains with its provinces having an average poverty incidence of 50 per cent in 1994 and representing among the poorest in the country.

Another challenge that has emerged is how government can sustain the interest of the MNLF in the peace process. With the new organic act in place, the SPCPD was already being targeted for abolition, along with other government agencies that had no legal mandates, but were created to help boost development efforts in Mindanao. Yet the ARMM only covered Muslim-dominated areas.

To be sure, it certainly looks like Mindanao will remain a tough nut to crack for most presidents. President Arroyo not only has to deal with the renewed ferment among the secessionist rebels, she also has to deal with the proliferation of kidnap for ransom gangs which have made Mindanao even more "off-limits" to investments, it seems. Yet the more I read about new problems, the more I became convinced that, contrary to the defeatist line that little can be done "in a place like that," Mindanao should represent an opportunity for leaders to show their political will to eradicate poverty to pursue sustainable human development.

When I first pushed for involvement of the UNDP in Mindanao, our staff was split right down the middle between those who wanted it and those who didn't. Both Sarah Timpson and I were scared about taking a big risk. The risks became greater when we started to call in the donors. By involving more people, we ran the risk of having more people blame us later if something goes wrong, and corollary, of opening more people to the risk of failure—with the possibility that, if "burned," they might withdraw completely.

But now, if I'm asked on hindsight if I would take the risks again, I will not hesitate to say yes.

Looking back on my more than two years of involvement in Mindanao, there are a few things that I can think we could have done better. We should have worked harder on the relationship with the government, especially the local government. Particularly, we're seeing that in Sarangani and General Santos. The election of Muslimin Sema as mayor of Cotabato City and of Yusop Jikiri as governor of Sulu mirrors a significant improvement as well. Both were former top lieutenants of Misuari.

Maybe we should really invest more attention in local executives in Mindanao, rather than in Manila. The same is true with the mass media, which is unfortunately too centralized in Metro Manila. I don't think we have been listening very well to the voice of the local mass media.

Finally, perhaps we should have paid more attention to relations with the Organization of Islamic Conference (OIC), which has supported the peace progress in Mindanao. There should be a more balanced picture—that the

UN does not just work for the industrialized countries or organizations but is also a bigger partner for the OIC.

Paul Oquist, the UNDP's senior regional-governance adviser for Asia, in leading four assessment missions in Mindanao said that, indeed, "a window of opportunity exists for peace and development in Mindanao."

But, he warns, "this brilliant window of opportunity faces serious risk. This is the case of the point that the policy process is now at a critical inflection point. Either the peace and development process moves ahead within the favorable political window of opportunity, or it breaks down politically."

Mr. Oquist cites the implications of a political breakdown of the process.

"1. The extreme protraction of the conflict with both increased political violence and worst case scenarios already visible on the ground (i.e. the proliferation of "lost commands" and other kidnap-for-ransom groups)"

"2. The loss of political and physical climate necessary to make foreign direct investment the solution to the economic constraints of the peace process"

"3. The discrediting of autonomy for peace and development as the solution in the southern Philippines after over 25 years of efforts to construct it as such, and the concomitant creation of a high threshold of difficulty for reviving the discredited process in the future."

Indeed, there were other "marginalized" groups that were alienated, and these have become a major concern for confidence building in Mindanao. While there is a final peace agreement with the MNLF and the 15 state commanders are cooperating with government, emerging as the biggest threat was the Moro Islamic Liberation Front, which continued to wage an armed struggle.

As this was being written, Nur Misuari has also declared a "revolt" of such sorts, and at dawn on November 18, 2001, was accused by the military of ordering the attacks on various government installations in Sulu province.

His apparent motive is to stop the holding of the ARMM elections on November 26.

Meanwhile, there were rumblings in the MNLF leadership. Misuari, who had become the rallying figure during the MNLF's armed struggle and the transition years, suddenly found himself isolated from the MNLF leadership. He was suddenly named chairman emeritus, but his powers and the leadership of the organization were taken over by a 15-man council, including his most trusted political lieutenants.

While Misuari maintained his mandate as ARMM governor, the SPCPD was chaired by its executive director Muslimin Sema, himself elected an elected mayor in Cotabato City and one of the prime movers of the new council of leaders.

Mr. Sema has proposed the setting up of an Office for SZOPAD concerns, knowing that the abolition of the SPCPD could giver wrong signals to their former combatants. There were issues, he noted, that remain uncertain: "What are the alternatives for SZOPAD and SPCPD, two implementing mechanisms provided in the final peace agreement, which the new organic act will abolish? What if the MNLF cannot accept the law as the ultimate implementation of the final peace agreement?"

The Oquist report, noted that the existing conduit for the MNLF support is the SPCPD. "It has the accumulated experience in dealing with the demobilization of politico-military organization structures. It also has a positive working experience in dealing with the demobilization of politico-military organization structures. It also has established a positive working relationship with the two principal donors who have supported that process, the UNDP-led Multidonor Support Group and USAID."

It was a move that was aimed to slowly repair the crack not only within the MNLF leadership—but also on how they can actively participate in the peace process. After his supporters were accused of barricading a government complex in Zamboanga City, Misuari and several aides escaped to Malaysia, but were arrested and deported weeks later. He is in detention in Laguna, a province south of Metro Manila, and is on trial for the Zamboanga City raid. But the MNLF leadership in general continued to assure that they would respect the peace pact.

Despite the gains in confidence-building efforts through the multidonor program, institutionalizing the peace may not come overnight.

As Mr. Oquist has observed: "The conflict and its causes will not be easily forgotten. The stakeholders continue to need education about peace process and help with learning non-violent and effective techniques of conflict resolution and cultural co-existence."

CHAPTER 8

TROUBLE IN PARADISE

The donors who responded to our call for a coordinated, multilateral-bilateral approach to the postconflict rehabilitation of the Muslim Mindanao region needed little prodding because many of them had either; been involved in Mindanao for years, albeit in different undertakings; or had been closely watching events there, and were anxious to help make a difference and prove that peace has its dividends.

From where my colleagues and I sat at the UNDP, we had deliberately planned our involvement in Mindanao with a view to harnessing, for the first time in years, the kind of capacity and expertise that the UN had built up through the years in postconflict resolution, in peace and development work and in aid coordination.

From where they—the donor governments and institutions—sat, I presumed that they would be eager to make a stake in the place, considering the international interest that this peace breakthrough had generated. But as with all big undertakings that involve a lot of people and resources, the first few weeks were quite challenging.

To be sure, it had always been my style to reinforce my office-hours encounters with colleagues in the development assistance community with some personal, after-office casual sessions. Gerry McGovern of the European Union used to complain that I had an unbelievable stamina level, especially when I would invite people for a couple of beers even at past 9 or 10 at night, after a long day's work or a marathon meeting.

Besides beer sessions, Gerry and I shared a passion for golf. But Gerry never seemed to mind even if our professional concerns would intrude into our conversations over beer or about golf. He would tell me later he appreciated that kind of an approach.

One other reason why he and I easily appreciated each other's approach and strategies was that we both had worked quite extensively in Africa.

Much later also, Lyn Pieper of the Australian Agency for International Development (AusAid) would say that she appreciated the informal meetings and dinners, especially the one I hosted in January 1997, which most donor representatives would consider as our group's "graduation" of sorts before we all plunged headlong into Mindanao.

Gerry McGovern attended that dinner in my house the day after he came back from Cotabato, where he said he was impressed by what he saw and heard, especially after talking to a very determined Muslimin Sema, Nur Misuari's point man, and the leaders of the Bangsa Moro women working with the MNLF, including Nur's wife; as well as the Cabinet of the Autonomous Region in Muslim Mindanao (ARMM).

Gerry highlighted the challenge rather eloquently: "In Mindanao, there's more than enough work for everybody."

So there we were, about seven outsiders meeting in a house in the financial center of Makati City, trying to make sense of our roles as so-called development experts, in a place as promising but also as unpredictable as Mindanao. We were, I guess, trying to balance our enthusiasm to help, with our well-reasoned conviction that none of us should come along and pray God with the people of Mindanao—neither could we afford even being remotely suspected of doing so.

The Philippine government had asked us all to take Mindanao seriously, and from as far as we can remember, we tried to do that. For my part, all I could bring to the table was, besides my unique personal experience in conflict resolution in Sudan, the UN's own wealth of experience in mediating conflicts in such places as Guatemala and Mozambique. Moreover, I also brought to the table the wish of the UNDP office in Manila to make this thing work while reinventing itself into a more dynamic, more activist kind of development organization.

AusAid Lyn Pieper best reflects the sense of humility

that infused most of us gathered around that table in January 1997. Years before the September 1996 peace agreement, many of the countries represented by the people there in my house had been involved in Mindanao one way or another. But hearing Lyn make sense of that meeting later, I realize now that perhaps the multilateral-bilateral program in Mindanao took off because, although several of the players involved had certain ideas about what their countries could do given their respective foreign policies or development assistance philosophies, everyone was prepared to make some changes based on what we would all collectively find out about the needs of the ex-combatant communities-needs that they themselves, the local population, enunciated.

"The informal meetings and dinners, like that dinner, were really an avenue for all of us to discuss openly what our concerns were, what the complexities of the problem were, what role each of us might actually have to play; what is one donor good at, and the other donor is good for," Lyn Pieper would recall later.

She would add another plus from those interactions; intelligence gathering—and then explains; A lot of the donors had been involved somehow in Mindanao, but the situation has been evolving, and each one should be quickly attuned to changes to remain relevant. "What is unsafe this month might be perfectly safe the next month. So we don't have any official ban on working in particular areas. We just try and tract the security situation regularly.

We do have our own expertise and our own intelligence and own contacts within Mindanao, but I still find that there's much I could get from UNDP which is very valuable to add to that."

Gerry McGovern looks back on the experience this way: "There are pockets of assistance spread all around the MNLF area. We were all working towards a common goal of establishing confidence, because there was a lot of suspicion in Mindanao. We were making a contribution to nation building while waiting for the government to do something. The donors can only be catalysts for action, we can't respond to everything. In effect, we were buying time until the government has a chance to do something."

Although he had not attended that January 1997 dinner in my house, one other donor representative who played a key role in the Mindanao program was Hideaki Harada, first secretary of the Japanese Embassy in the Philippines. Like Gerry and me, Hideaki has also worked in Africa (Tanzania, South Africa) and thus had a clear sense of what we were up against.

Before the 1996 peace agreement, Japan had been an active development partner of the Philippines. Hideaki notes with pride that even after the Asian crisis started to make its impact felt in the Philippines, Japanese investment in the Philippines, "particularly in the economic zones," had been maintained; and that Japan remained the top donor in the Philippines, "providing about 60 percent of the foreign ODA (Official Development Assistance)."

In Japan's view, he says, "ODA and private sector investment is [the best form of] support to Philippine economic development."

When a call was made for donors to close ranks with the UN in some sort of a comprehensive postconflict program for Mindanao, Hideaki says the Japanese government responded quickly, although "our projects are not limited to the MNLF. We [just] provide assistance for communities, not specific groups."

He explains: Japanese ODA policy says assistance should target all recipients or nationals, not special groups; taxpayers' money should benefit as many as possible. Still, he adds, there was a conscious policy to give emphasis to Mindanao programs after the 1996 peace agreement. Right after the signing of the accord, or about the last quarter of 1996, we in the UNDP and the Japanese embassy met and soon the Japanese foreign minister issued a statement that the Japanese government supported Mindanao development. Hideaki recalls: "The clear project plan was not ready when the announcement was read. But in October, we dispatched a mission to hold political dialogues with the Philippines government on how to cooperate on the SPCPD (Southern Philippines Council for Peace and Development). Since then, we have sent out economic cooperation missions to Davao, Cotabato and Zamboanga."

In effect, the Japanese tack was different from Australia or the EU in the sense that it did not focus specifically on the MNLF. But it did increase the level of assistance and attention to Mindanao, with the long-term view of sustaining an atmosphere conducive to peace and development.

Hideaki cites examples of this approach: "During the shortage brought about by El Nino, the EU and other donors granted cash to procure food. We don't have such kind of cash contribution. Our current projects are more of grant programs. One involves the provision of heavy construction equipment in order to build roads, bridges and other infrastructure in Western Mindanao. The other is an anti-malarial program, where we provide mosquito nets to Western Mindanao and Palawan. Our contributions are not tied with Japanese products, and depend on competitive bidding."

Hideaki estimates that more than US$300,000 has been disbursed in Japanese aid for the entire Philippines. According to him, it has been his government's policy to channel much of the ODA through the annual package of 140 billion Japanese yen, 90 percent of which is coursed through the Philippine government. The ODA channeled through NGOs is about 150 million Japanese yen, which goes mostly to grassroots projects.

While the construction and antimalaria programs are projects of the Japan International Cooperation Agency (Jica), grassroots assistance projects are handled by the Embassy itself. Hideaki echoes Pieper's observation about the UNDP playing the crucial role of helping donors get a clearer sense of what's going on in Mindanao, so that their assistance could have more focus. "In other Asian countries," he notes, "we usually have sufficient information on economic and social development. But in the case of Mindanao we had almost nothing.

Before 1996, he adds, most of the assistance in Mindanao were "small-scale grants," reflecting the cautious attitude in a place that seemed as unpredictable as ever. "Before the peace accord and before UNDP's involvement we were cautious, we had no assurance that the ODA would be spent properly, and we had no contact for any Concrete project, especially with the central government and the Muslim groups fighting each other (a few years before the 1996 peace agreement, a breakaway MNLF faction had formed the MILF or Moro Islamic Liberation Front). But now there is certainty, with NEDA, etc." The EU tack in Mindanao hued closely to the three-phase formula that the UNDP more or less adopted; confidence building and "buying time" to help stabilize the postconflict situation; emergency relief; and livelihood and long-term development. For postconflict rehab and emergency aid, the EU drew from a long history in Africa, says Gerry McGovern. Meanwhile, it had a similar experience in going from immediate relief to long-term development in the Philippines itself, in Northern Luzon after the killer earthquake of 1990.

But Gerry is even more emphatic than I am about the need to maintain, first of all, a certain level of confidence in peace. "You've to have peace in order to develop our region. We have to act quickly in order to stabilize peace. It is very fragile. On my first exploratory trip to Cotabato in 1997, I'd hear people say, "Well, if nothing happens to us, we'll just go back to the hills."

He lays down the line of the EU in no uncertain terms: "We in the EU believe that without peace in Mindanao, there will be no peace in the Philippines. Without peace there will be no investments; and there will be no economic and social development. So it's very logical cycle, and all the parts have to be in place. We've seen that in Africa, Central America—without peace, you can't have social development."

Lyn Pieper sees the peace building process as being critical to Australia's long-term vision to see Mindanao develop its maximum potential—critical not only for the SZOPAD, but all other parts of Mindanao as well. Australia, after all, she notes, has been very active in the peace building process and postconflict resolution in Cambodia. Still, she says the Mindanao situation is a challenge unto itself. It is distinguished "by the fact that the conflict had gone on for so long and the people down there (Mindanao) had been so isolated—not just geographically, but also politically, most of them in very remote areas. And there are the various complexities that go with the links with the OIC, what that means for the future development of Mindanao. There was the question of 'did Muslim Mindanao want to be seen to be part of the global Muslim community, or did it want to be seen to be part of the Philippine community?' That required careful planning, policy development."

While complaining about the dearth of information on the evolving situation in Mindanao before the UN put together the multi-bi programme for Mindanao, Lyn Pieper notes that Australia has actually been involved in the past in certain key areas in the South (three of the six cities where they're in are Iligan, Cagayan de Oro and General Santos). "But the real formal decision to focus on Mindanao was made in 1996.

Once the official Mindanao multi-bi programme was put in place, Lyn recalls, "we at AusAid were confident the UN would be able to implement it successfully [because] they've already done all the ground work and done it quite extensively." She was referring to the fact that even before the formal needs assessment survey began in 1997, the UNDP was down in Mindanao talking to Muslim communities, to the MNLF, to women, tribal people building rapport with the people on the ground.

And now, from the looks of it, the donors would have to be involved in Mindanao for a possibly much longer period than they had originally planned. It takes years, as Gerry McGovern notes, before an investment idea translates into jobs. It takes years to put in place good, permanent infrastructure; and it takes years of on again, off again, peace negotiations and dialogues to convince all stakeholders that no matter what happens, there should be no giving up on the peace process.

Since we in the UN issued our terminal report on the "SPCPD-UN-NEDA Programme" that ran from 1997 to 1998, many things have taken place that shook confidence in the ability of the peace process to endure. The government and the MILF have been unable to buckle down finally to formal peace negotiations beyond declaring temporary cease-fires that have been disrupted at least twice. This conflict inevitably spills over into the MNLF areas, affecting earlier gains in peacebuilding.

I asked Gerry recently if he thought the donor effort has provoked greater government action, and his candid reply was that he honestly had no substantial information on what the Philippines government had done. "I just hope that the government would be less modest and come out and say what it has done. Some of the people of Nur Misuari say the government has not delivered. The government should make an effort to explain what it has done," Gerry says, adding that this process of explaining contributes to building confidence.

In other words, from his succinct declaration, in late 1996 when we first got involved in Mindanao, the slogan "In Mindanao, there's enough work for everyone" has now become even more challenging: "The work is never really done."

From Paradise Lost to Paradise Regained, the one certain thing about Mindanao nowadays is that it's a paradise in perpetual peril from trouble. Does this mean we all gambled on the wrong place, the wrong people, and the wrong cause? Far from it. It simply bears out, yet again, the challenge that the UN and the donor community perpetually faces everytime they attempt to help out in a troubled spot anywhere in the world. Perhaps if we had not worked in Africa, or Mongolia, or witnessed the UN's saga in Cambodia, we would have said, "Mindanao is hopeless." But until this day, I think I can fairly assume that everyone who brought down on the table their bets for peace, in that long dinner in January 1997, remains convinced we did the right thing.

For the record, the whole effort mobilized more than $10 million for the postconflict program. Certainly, not everything can continue to be sourced from donors. But to the extent that this initial funding has helped sustain a climate of peace and started former warriors on the road to peace, at least the potential for luring investors remains.

Of all the things that we've done in Mindanao, I think one crucial point—an observation that Hideaki, Gerry and Lyn made separately—is that the UN system's unprecedented foray into Mindanao has helped demystify the place, etching out for all to see the real dangers and challenges while bringing to the fore the risk potential for development of the place and its people. If I may indulge in my favorite African experience, it was like going into the bush once again, but this time, seeing the thick foliage cleared, the myth separated from reality. Knowing—and seeing what's ahead—has removed the mystery, and with it, at least half of the fear of failing.

Most important of all, we met, saw, and for several scattered brief moments, lived with a people grown tired of war; people who were passionately devoted to making peace work. In the MNLF state structures, we saw, not just an organization for dividing people into combat commands, but one that functioned as well as a community map—with built-in features for exercising responsible leadership, for consultations, for a representative form of decision making. In truth, these were features that made it possible for the UN-donors' team and the Philippines government to tap the existing MNLF state structure as the vehicle for the first and second phases of the 18-month peace and development project in Mindanao.

Because we have helped clear a path, I hope the investors and other parties with a means to continue where we began would take that path and assume the challenge of development.

Besides the psychic satisfaction of having faced squarely the challenge in Mindanao, I am most gratified by the thought that this undertaking has helped put the UN back on track—at least in this part of the world—as a credible, capable coordinator for development; and the UNDP, as a catalytic agent emphasizing the building of human and institutional capacity among Mindanao's former warrior communities and their local governments.

In a sense, the Philippine experience was different from Africa because we were not actually in the middle of a war in Mindanao, but it was important that efforts be maintained to sustain the fragile peace. Relatively, we worked around with little money, but the littleness of that amount may have been an asset. If we had so much money, we may have had problems of absorptive capacity. We were forced to be creative and innovative with the meager resources that we had, and that's what is supposed to make the UN system unique.

Money was important but it was not the primary concern in rebuilding Mindanao's war-torn areas. With money should come the message that we all have confidence in the local population and recognize their efforts to build a just society for themselves; and, in turn, we must earn their respect and their trust. We must send the message that only by being self-reliant in the long term, can they be able to chart their own destiny as they see fit.

As I said earlier, the Mindanao challenge came at a time when I was deep into trying to reinvent the UNDP's Manila office, getting people more involved in the field than just in passive research work; in a more comprehensive view of development rather than just each one's narrow concerns. The idea to do both—reinventing the office and facing the challenge of peace and development in Mindanao—was, it seems now, a divinely inspired idea that has brought me the deepest satisfaction from my UNDP-Manila experience.

Lyn Pieper says one reason why she pushed hard for Australia to be involved in the Mindanao program was because she did not want to "try to use it as a model for UN coordination, for coordination in the UN system itself. I thought that was very, very valuable."

Indeed, if Lyn only knew how valuable that has become to me, both in a personal and professional sense, after all these years. I prepared to leave the Philippines with the strong need for reassurance; that those who remained in Mindanao would continue to see and do things through that prism—that peace comes before development, even as long-term development is the best guarantee for sustaining peace, and that there will always be enough work for everyone.

CHAPTER 9

ONE GLANCE BACKWARD, ONE STEP FORWARD

In my dealings, in my relationships, I am always direct. In my career, I always want to go forward, reach farther. But my life seems to be a series of desires and situations that meander and twist, most of them eventually coming full circle.

Remember how excited I was back then in 1980 when I was told of my first assignment: Bhutan. Though there wasn't much that I knew about it, one thing was for sure: the thought of this tiny kingdom—and its breathtaking gorges and notoriously lethal rapids, its relative isolation and its tenacious hold on old traditions—caught my imagination.

Had it not been for that more urgent call to Uganda, Bhutan would have been my first posting. But no matter. As I got ready to leave my post as Deputy Res. Rep. in the Philippines, I welcomed the thought of finally reaching Bhutanese soil on my seventh posting, this time as UN Resident Representative.

It was anybody's guess as to whether I would be coming in at a good or bad time, although personally, I was not very much bothered by the possibility of coming in at an awkward time. After all, life has consistently brought me to each of my postings at some of the most interesting times (to put it very mildly). And all these, together with my experiences in the concrete jungles of Tokyo and Washington and New York and other cities, have seemingly been for the purpose of keeping me in a healthy cycle of learning and unlearning.

It seemed propitious that I would cap two decades of development work in such diverse places by serving as UNDP Resident Representative in this tiny kingdom nestled in the Himalayas, a land of gentle and intelligent people; and unparalleled and—one hopes, perpetually—unspoiled beauty, Bhutan.

Propitious, indeed, and ironic, too, because Bhutan had

nowhere near the scale of conflict and unpredictable tensions that I saw in much of Africa, or in the Sudan where two wars, tribe against tribe and humanity against hunger, seemed to be the perpetual order of the day. Also, Bhutan had neither the complex challenges of a giant in transition as China was after the crucible called Tiananmen in 1994; or of a tiny corner called Mindanao in the Philippines, where nurturing a fragile peace after nearly three decades of strife had been the UN's most distinct undertaking.

As I would eventually find out however, Bhutan, for all its near-legendary beauty and the allure of its deeply Buddhist lifestyle posed its own peculiar challenges when I got on board as resident representative (and concurrently as UN resident coordinator) in 1999. In a sense, Bhutan's situation had parallels with Mongolia, which was beginning to democratize and thus was the scene of tremendous changes when Hiroko and I arrived there in the 80's.

By the time I was completing *Footpaths & Highways* (the first edition of this book), Hiroko and I were also busy preparing to move to Bhutan, and by the time we arrived the nation itself was much absorbed in its own preparations.

June 1999 was marked by great festivity because King Jigme Singye Wangchuck, who had ascended the Golden Throne in 1974 (the year he was formally crowned), was marking the Silver Jubilee of such ascension. It was a time of widespread joy for the nation that deeply loved its leader, its head of state and government, also known as the

Druk Gyalpo (Dragon King).

Despite the indisputably strong base of support he enjoyed, however, the king himself insisted that all events related to his Silver Jubilee be meaningful and not ostentatious. This insistence stemmed from precisely that sensitivity and strength of character that had compelled him to bravely dare and take his country through the risky currents of opening up to the world.

King Jigme Singye Wangchuck had succeeded his father, Jigme Dorji Wangchuck, upon the latter's death in 1972, which was, incidentally, just a year after Bhutan was formally accepted as a UN member.

At that time, King Jigme Singye Wangchuck had become the world's youngest monarch. Yet even at that tender age the Britain and India-educated ruler already showed an unusually keen grasp of the essence of participative and consultative governance, as he would, early on in his reign, take his entire family on an eight-month tour of the entire kingdom, stopping by every village and farm, talking to everyone he saw, listening to both the things that bothered them or gave them joy. Early on he had also made known his unbreakable rule; that no subject who comes to see him should ever be turned away.

Indeed, a lot of the achievements of the UN in that kingdom which I will discuss later could be traced in great measure to the unstinting cooperation of the King, who provided the clear vision for the future he had in mind for Bhutan, and encouraged ordinary citizens to make known their own aspirations whenever possible.

The monarch proved himself to be well beyond a narrow vision of a supreme patriarch who alone could solve the problems of the kingdom. He had, in his own way, institutionalized participative governance; and more importantly, he had lain the groundwork for the formation and strengthening of institutions by which the citizens' views and efforts could be marshaled in an organized manner.

The King had planned the decentralization and democratization as early as the 1980s, but again, with his sensitivity, designed it in such a way that changes would proceed in stages, to give people time to adjust and mature, and the institutions to evolve along with the people's maturing.

As recounted by *Kuensel* (Bhutan's national newspaper), "In 1981, he instituted the District Development Committee (DYT) to decentralize authority to the district (dzongkhag) level . This was taken to the village level with the establishment of block development committees (GYT) in 1991. In the same year he stepped down as chairman of the Planning Commission. In recent years the King has ensured that a representative from every family attended the development meetings in their districts.

"Having nurtured the system of governance into maturity, he bestowed full executive powers to an elected team which he himself groomed."

This happened in 1998 at the height of his reign and popularity. King Wangchuck handed over the reins of governance to his people, dissolved a long-standing Cabinet, introduced an elected term for Ministers, and transferred full executive powers to the new elected Cabinet. In one fell swoop, he introduced accountability, participation and representation, and transparency to the affairs of state.

According to Kuensel, the King tried to assuage the protests that initially erupted from those who opposed the changes, while easing the fears of many citizens scared by what it all would lead to, with these words, addressed to the shocked Cabinet that was given full executive powers: "This is a special day for me. I truly believe that the new policies and changes will benefit the nation and the people. I am happy because I know that what I have done is in the best interests of my country and people."

Moreover, Kuensel takes note that "the depth of the decentralization policy lies in the emphasis on education which receives about 12 percent of the overall government budget. With nearly every eligible child in school, the King envisions an educated society with the ability to make responsible decisions....To those who still tend to look at the monarch as the one and only symbol of rule, this well-educated leader surprises everyone with the view that `the future of the country cannot be left in the hands of one individual. We must always give more importance to building the institution.' "

On hindsight, this selfless, visionary attitude was a pivotal factor in whatever success we (that is, the UN, myself, and all of Bhutan's development partners) had in guiding the process of change. It gave us the blanket guarantee, at every turn, that Bhutan would not—despite the difficulties and setbacks—ever go back from the path it had taken when it opened up to the world. It assured us that balanced development and good governance would go hand in hand with fostering Bhutan's Buddhist values amid the intricacies of building and steering a nation in the world of the Internet and globalization.

This last assurance was perhaps even more important to the Bhutanese themselves. It seemed as if among the many complex challenges that tested the resolve of this young, much-respected and progressive monarch, foremost was the question of which was the best, most balanced response to the mixed reactions of his people.

There were reactions not only to the internal governmental changes, but perhaps more critically, to the King's initiatives towards expansion and deepening of external relations (including its increasingly active role in the community of nations in the UN), and the consequent influx of external cultures and global economic realities.

Bhutan is a country of tremendous natural wealth owing to its rulers' conservative policies on exploitative and extractive economic activities. It's probably the only country where, because of strict forestry laws, the forest cover is increasing. Yet for all the beauty of Bhutan's natural resources and its most important treasure—a people with the distinct identity of being the last truly Buddhist society—the forces spawned by globalization were felt in the innermost corners of the kingdom. Understandably, there were and still are certain concerns about the country's ability to manage the long-term effects of globalization; there remain, among the Bhutanese, "conservatives" who wanted the country to open slowly—more slowly than the King himself had planned and allowed.

Its more controversial and volatile neighbor Nepal—and the "giants" China and India—looked on with a great deal of interest at this kingdom, which had a land mass 30 percent that of Nepal and less than two percent that of India. Right before their very eyes, Bhutan was becoming a stable and growing economy that could provide its 600,000 subjects with free education and free health services. I found it most interesting how a country like Bhutan, sandwiched as it was between the two "giants", developed its superb diplomatic skills.

Thus, right when Bhutan was deep in the cusp of a transition that had started two decades back, I arrived to begin the new phase of my journey as a development worker.

It seemed even the outer, physical qualities of my new posting were designed to clearly mark the boundaries between my old and the new postings.

From noisy, dirty, congested, warm Manila, I arrived at the Palo International Airport in Bhutan, one of the few airports in the world that still use visual landing systems. I was immediately welcomed by Bhutan's clean, crisply cold air, and received by Mr. Kesang Wangdi, chief of protocol,

Ministory of Foreign Affairs. I was served butter tea, similar to what Mongolians serve. My wife Hiroko and my son Keiichiro (who was four years old at that time) arrived together. My son was puzzled; he didn't know where he had landed.

From the Palo Airport to Thimphu, the capital, I took a long, winding two-hour trip.

My first impression was that this was a lovely country, although I felt that the expectations from UNDP were much higher than in all other countries that I had served.

Bhutan has a well-deserved reputation for being one of the most unspoilt corners on earth. The Bhutanese take special pride in saying that their forest cover is increasing while the rest of the world is hard put trying to save whatever little they still have. Credit must go to the national consensus, as reflected in policy, that, being a tiny country with an equally small population, and sandwiched by giants—in the political, economic and military sense—Bhutan's strength must lie in its ability to move steadily toward self-reliance, and that can be done partly by a judicious stewardship of its natural resources.

For all its natural resources, Bhutan is classified as a Least Developed Country (LDC), however, and while its people may take pride in having evolved the concept of "Gross National Happiness" as an alternative to the usual measurements of national wealth, still, it has its own peculiar challenge of poverty to overcome.

It has an agricultural, developing economy with strong

ties to India—part accident of location and part historical relationship. Industrial activity is limited (less than 1 percent of the population is involved in industrial work) and services—mainly because of its tourism potential—is a promising engine of growth. Some economic experts have focused on the need to develop its substantial hydroelectric capabilities both for domestic use and export. However, this—along with any other activity that impacts on the environment—is weighed very carefully in a country where resource conservation is a cornerstone policy.

When I came in 1999, the momentum for change was at its peak, as the kingdom started to take several bold steps to embrace globalization. The leaders knew that foreign aid—once close to 100 percent from India, later shifting to European countries and international multilateral organizations (more than 70 percent)—could not indefinitely be relied on to finance economic development.

Agriculture (including fishing and forestry), where an estimated 87 percent of the population is involved, accounts for nearly half of the GDP. The country is traditionally self-sufficient in food production, and has in fact been sending a lot of its students for agricultural studies and training in other Asian countries, but rice imports increased in the late 1980s. The agricultural research and development is important, because, with less than 6 percent of land cultivable, farm efficiency is a gospel. Corn and rice are the major crops, with oranges, apples and cardamoms topping the cash crops. Livestock is raised throughout the kingdom. This is supplemented by the output from fresh water and hatchery fishing.

The lumber industry accounts for roughly 15 percent of GDP, but as I stressed early on, stewardship of the forests (Bhutan boasts of 70 percent forest cover) is regarded as almost like a priesthood.

With a quarter of GDP accounted for by industry, the most basic industries are handicrafts, cement, food processing, wood milling and distilling; 400 small-scale cottage and industrial units complement these. Limestone, used for cement production, is a major mining and quarrying product.

Nearly a third of the GDP is accounted for by services, mainly in tourist-oriented commercial services and domestic-oriented wholesale and retail trade. Tourism stood as the largest foreign-exchange earner (US$2 million in 1987).

India, its giant neighbor, hogs much of foreign trade. The kingdom's exports in 1990 totaled 1.2 billion Nu—primarily, electricity and processed raw materials. Total imports, mostly rice and manufactured goods, totalled 1.8 billion Nu in 1990.

The kingdom through the years slowly corrected its trade imbalances, slowly shifting the ratio from a high of 80 percent imports and 20 percent exports in the 1980s, to a 60-40 imports-exports balance in the 90s.

The shifting ratio coincided with the deliberate efforts to start opening up the economy in the late 1980s, perhaps proving that opening up need not mean a surge of imports; instead, it could spur productivity and competitiveness.

It was against a background of continuing, exciting change that I again found myself when I first flew to Bhutan. It struck me as such a strong coincidence that I would always find myself so situated in all of my postings. But as I said, while Bhutan did not have the raw drama of Africa's wars and the political conflicts in China or Mindanao, it posed its own unique challenges. And as UNDP Resident Representative and concurrent UN resident coordinator, I was soon sucked right into the very vortex of its development.

In Bhutan, the UNDP is not just a development service organization, it is now perceived as the principal adviser for foreign policymaking as well.

As UN resident coordinator, I also approached the government, primarily the Ministry of Foreign Affairs, and asked them to shift their eye away from the region in the south, but to look far beyond, to the so-called Asean.

We deliberately encouraged the bringing in to Bhutan of and continuing exchanges with Asean experts—and for the Bhutanese to sometimes simply to visit or call on, or to explore Asean training institutions. This is still happening now.

The UN resident coordinator's de facto role as policy adviser extended to the thorny issue of tens of thousands of Bhutanese refugees in Nepal was also often discussed. I was asked to advise the government on how we should explore options for various fronts on these issues.

While the issues were different, I found a common thread between my experience in Bhutan and in the Philippines. In UNDP-Philippines, I worked quite hard to break barriers, bringing in Mindanao into the office, both to support the peace and development program after the 1996 peace agreement, as well as to encourage teamwork among the staff. In Bhutan, I resolved to undertake more or less the same approach, i.e., helping the UNDP staff, as well as the UN agencies, work more closely in facilitating the resolution by their Bhutanese counterparts of the pressing political and socioeconomic issues.

As is my style, I started with a "map" and used my first few weeks in this new territory to enhance and refine that map by getting a good grasp of the people who would help me use it. That is, I also went around and talked to each member of the staff, and then to our other partners in the UN agencies.

I prepared a Vision Document the day I arrived. The document kicks in through workshops 1,2 and 3; it emphasizes the long-running thread through my career—; teamwork and group performance rather than individual achievement. That, I was convinced then, is the UN management culture.

In managing the UNDP office, the vision document I prepared sought to put in place an office environment where:

- Staff can accept change and can respond promptly and successfully to new situations (interactive with changing environment).
- Constraints of the strict hierarchical organization are either refrained and/or eliminated (delegation/decentralization).
- Communication among all units is increased regardless of functions and of locations (information/intelligence gathering, analysis and sharing).
- Group performance rather than individual achievement would be encouraged (teamwork).

The Vision Document also expected staff to

- Continue to learn about the plans, needs and strength of the office (learning).
- Participate actively in the work and direction of the office (proactive and participative).
- Accept ownership of problems on behalf of the office (accountability).
- Expand their technical skills and master new ones (technological aspect).
- Share experience and knowledge with the larger group (transparency and differentiation).

The Vision Document encouraged everyone to look at the changing environment within and surrounding the UN/UNDP. I highlighted the greater number and variety of channels for taking actions and exerting influence (civil society, donors, private sectors, government, etc.); the shifts in relationships of influence from the vertical to the horizontal, from chain of command to peer networks (delegation/decentralization); the slowly diminishing distinction between managers and those managed especially in terms of information, control over assignments and access to internal and external relations (information technology and human relations/interaction). External relations have become increasingly important as sources of internal power and influence. Finally, the Vision Document stressed that our client needs are changing and UN/UNDP must stay relevant to the changing environment. To help our office implement our competitive organizational strategies, we must learn, the Document added, new ways to manage, confronting changes of our own power, and reorganize the need for new ways to motivate people (Ref. Prof David A. Garvin "Building a Learning Organization", *Harvard Business Review*, July–August, 1993).

One section of the Vision Document dwells on "The Bases of Power (How Our Office Continues To Be Relevant)." I quote here the highlights of that portion:

- Success depends increasingly on tapping into sources of good ideas, on figuring out whose collaboration is needed to act on those ideas, on working with both to produce results.
- Cross-boundary programmes like poverty, environment, governance, etc. centered on "Sustainable Human Development" are designed to encourage process con-

sultations with the stakeholders of UN/UNDP.
- The ability of managers to get things done depends on the number of networks in which they are centrally involved than on their height in a hierarchy (not control but empowerment).
- In an emerging office, we have to add value by deal-making, by brokering at interface, rather than by presenting over their individual authority (human relations and negotiation skills).
- Every staff member must think cross-functionally because every unit has to play a strategic role, understanding and contributing to other phases of the work (i.e., programmes of poverty, environment, governance and economic development, etc. are to complement the cross-boundary activities, including the UN system's collaboration).
- The office should seek problem-solving and initiative-taking staff who will go the unexpected extra mile for the client (willingness to take additional responsibilities).
- The new loyalty may not be to the boss or to the system but perhaps to programmes and projects that actualize a mission of UN/UNDP and offer challenge, growth and credit to results (innovation and programme development and performance).

Thus armed with a Vision Document, I confidently went about my first few days at UNDP Bhutan talking to everyone—UN staff and Bhutanese alike. By nature, the Bhutanese people are, with their religion and other beliefs, very harmonious and accommodating, but it takes them a lot to open up, reminding me of my experience with Mongolians. I know that in some Oriental cultures, it takes time to open up, but when they do so, they become one's permanent friends.

When I arrived at the Office, I did what I did in the Philippines. I interviewed everyone on the staff, from the drivers up to the deputy resident representative, all 33 people. But this time I expanded to the UN system as well, so I probably interviewed 120 people and got a good idea of what's happening. I visited all the government agencies, talked to the directors; but I also interacted with the drivers from time to time.

The mutual trust and confidence forged through such intensive informal meetings was, I must say, very much appreciated. I heard from my staff later that not many Res-Reps would take as much time to reach out to the staff. From my experience of the last 20 years, without this intensive and sincere interaction to understand how the staff look at management, or perceive the organization, it will be difficult to find the right direction for the group's performance, and so doing gain mutual understanding and trust.

Indeed, the Bhutanese may not seem refined in terms of their sense of modernization, but certainly they're eager to learn. I thought that I should try to promote their potential. Whenever I went on a field trip, I would take 6-7 of our staff (composition of the team would be from messengers to program officers), and let them know what the UN system/UNDP is doing in their country.

Most said it's their first time to travel to see their own country. One staffer said it took nine years before he saw his own country outside of the capital. That was an eye opener for me. After the field trips, the productivity of the staff, and their confidence in me and the UN management rose substantially. This is their own country, their system, but bringing in local knowledge into the UN system/UNDP has been overlooked. Not bringing along the locals, one fails to exploit the national potential and allow them to blend with the management commitment.

The field trips were not the end. I rotated the staff. I convinced my assistant to assume the post of head of general services, by releasing her to the administration.

Some of these staff rotations are going on in view of the matrix management that I introduced in the year 2000 workshop II. Reflections on the capacity building gave our national staff an opportunity to work at the level of international assignments. Now, three national volunteers are serving in Kosovo operations as UNVs; two went to East Timor; and two to Eritrea.

On May 28, 2000, I convened the Palo Workshop 3, my last time to serve as resident representative of the UNDP in Bhutan. Sam Mueller, UN Volunteers Service officer from UNDP, and Philippine NGO leader Isagani Serrano ably facilitated the sessions. The Power Workshop 3 was a culmination of several important documents that we prepared throughout my stint as resident representative in Bhutan. There was the report on the 7th RT meeting on November 7-9, 2000 in Thimphu, the planning workshops for 1999 and year 2000, the annual resident representative's reports for 1999 and 2000 and of course, the Vision Document prepared in April 1999 on my arrival.

Much of the process involved in preparing these documents grew out of the UNDP's previous experience in countries undergoing similar change; there is a deliberate effort to involve the community in a participative process of identifying, then assessing their needs as well as the assets or resources they possess and can harness; and in listing the most pressing issues and challenges that they need to resolve to meet these needs.

I felt a certain thrill from knowing that here at least there was some firm consensus, if not unanimity, among the Bhutanese and the international community represented by the UN.

To my relief, much of the sensitive issues that I thought I should take up with the Royal Government of Bhutan (RGOB) had been laid down, right from the start, by the international donor partners during the planning workshops for 1999 and 2000 and most especially, in the Round Table Meeting in Thimphu in November, 2000. For the calm exterior of the country and the serenity of the people somehow masked the debates and the tug of war that went on, all the while I was there, between the "conservatives" and those officials who took to heart the King's policy of opening up to the farthest extent possible without harming the nation. The "conservatives" said they want the country to open up more slowly. That's alright if the intent is to preserve cultural tradition or values. But it soon became clear to me that they also wanted to clamp down on disclosures of important information like socioeconomic profiles, and other basic economic data vital to policy planners as well as multinational business investors. Until then, we didn't know how many minority groups and their respective populations were. Data on distribution of population were hard to get, prompting the UNFPA to hold an international population census.

The "conservatives" were also sensitive to the human rights issue, especially involving the ULFA/BODO militants and the refugees in Nepalese camps. There was no specific gender program. The regional disparities between the east, west, south were unknown, especially in terms of girls' education.

Bhutanese take pride in their "GNH" concept, which puts such intangibles as having clean air, a well-conserved environment, relatively little stress, access to basic services, and a sense of ownership in government among the sources of a people's "wealth" and well-being. In truth, however, Bhutan had not developed the kind of rigid, multidisciplinary strategy to determine the full and real picture of poverty. There was scant information on poverty in terms of basic data; and an even more scant information on regional disparities.

During the Seventh Round Table Meeting in Thimphu in 2000, Ms. Eimi Watanabe, UN Assistant Secretary General and Director of the Bureau of Development Policy, served as co-chairperson of the meeting. She praised the Bhutanese vision of GNH as something in total consonance with the UN's human-centered approach to development. But in the next breath she stressed the need to pursue the geog-level (block level or village) poverty study, citing how the unavailability of information had hamstrung the development of appropriate anti-poverty strategies.

The little information available at that time indicated, she said, significant disparities in poverty and other human development indicators among regions.

In comments on our Resident Coordinator's Annual Report for Bhutan in 2000, Ameerah Haq, Associate Director of the UN Development Group Office, underscored the need to prod Bhutan towards having a formal definition of poverty and setting a national poverty line. The GNH provides a "qualitative and holistic perspective on poverty, but does not provide sufficient quantitative analysis," said Ms. Haq. Such lack of quantitative information, she said, "makes it difficult to analyse the scope, causes and consequences of poverty." I was encouraged to have the UN Country Team in Bhutan implement the Memorandum of Understanding between the UNDP and the

ADB on conducting a baseline poverty assessment, "with a view to strengthening the basis for strategic choices."

Yet another sensitive issue, besides poverty and gender, was human rights, especially in connection with the handling of the ULFA/BODO militants and the refugees in Nepal. At the RTM, Ms. Watanabe kindly underscored how, besides Bhutan's commendable efforts at decentralization, good governance also entailed promoting human rights. She cited as basis the Millennium Summit declaration then just concluded in New York, mandating all nations "to strive for the full protection and promotion of civil, political, economic, social and cultural rights for their peoples." She expressed as well the UNDP commitment to help the RGOB in the reintegration of returnees.

To be fair, most of the Bhutanese officials I encountered fully embraced the King's policy of openness and transparency. As long as they're convinced we're moving in the interest of the government, and not our own interest, things were okay with them.

I myself felt very lucky to have access to the King and the entire royal family. It seemed that in many ways, he was more progressive than the younger bureaucrats. This kind of dilemma impelled my shift in strategy in those days, i.e., to focus on training more or drafting mid-level career bureaucrats rather than ministers level; and give them a chance to make their plans a reality.

During the RTM, one candid assessment I heard from a minister-level official was that provided by Lyonpo Kinzang Dorji, the agriculture minister, who chaired the session on poverty and infrastructure. Right at the start, he acknowledged that while abject poverty did not exist in the country, the full benefits of development had not reached certain areas. He conceded that pockets of vulnerable and disadvantaged groups suffered from relative deprivation, but stressed that the government was giving priority to poverty alleviation, promoting income-generating activities and boosting food security systems.

An analysis at the RTM on such indicators as the human development index, household income and food security, including land size and livestock holding, showed an average Bhutanese monthly income at only $46. Still, the country narrowly avoided being tagged "abject poor," as most households could subsist on their farm produce. Much of Bhutan, however, remained vulnerable to food insecurity as a result of natural disasters and climate factors, loss of crops to wildlife, pests and diseases, and its landlocked and isolated situation. In short, there was seasonal food insecurity although there was no chronic hunger. A FAO/UNDP study showed half of rural households encountered grain deficits.

Food distribution systems were hampered by the fact that while Bhutan had a good network of roads, land travel was the only means available for going around the country, and tiny as it may seem, it often took days to go from point to point. Moreover, while all the districts save one were connected, the road network had barely branched out to the rural areas. Hence, infrastructure development was seen as a pillar of economic development and poverty alleviation.

In between the planning workshops and the RTM and various other key meetings where the problems of infrastructure, food security, population and health, among others, were discussed, I later realized an uncanny coincidence; the work seemed more comprehensive and intense—could it have been because the agency heads of Unicef, FAO, World Food Program and WHO were all females?

Dealing with women agency heads taught me a lot, I now realize on hindsight. Sometimes we would have very detailed discussions, starting with the macro and ending up with the need to repair female toilets.

Besides having women agency heads, the gender ratio in the UN staff in Bhutan was a pleasant 65:35 percent female-male.

From experience, I could say that female workers are reliable, hardworking and trustworthy. But often I struggle to bring back their thinking to the mainstream. At times, my frustration is that they want to reopen discussions on something we've already agreed upon. That's something I never thought of, but maybe I have to understand that sometimes they're insecure or unsure about an idea and they want to reopen discussions.

Women, generally, also supported me in my coordination work, especially in drafting the UN Development Assistance Framework, in light of UN reforms; as well as in the Second Review for the UN Common Country Assessment (the only document that covers socioeconomic and political issues in the whole country).

It seemed propitious that the bulk of such coordination work would be provided by women, who seemed to understand instinctively the critical need for reforms in the UN system—from the standpoint of maximizing scarce resources, of encouraging more participative decision-making processes, and from giving primary, undivided focus to sustainable human development as the anchor of all development efforts.

CHAPTER
10

OPEN AT PERIL, STAY CLOSE AND DIE

A country committed to Gross National Happiness. Blessed with a rich cultural heritage, and a pristine environment. Bhutan has been projected as the Shangri-La of the Himalayas, but to say it is paradise or a perfect place is to misrepresent it.

It is also a Least Developed Country in terms of GDP per capita, but dealing with its pockets of poverty amid a generally happy and satisfied population requires a measure of opening up, of learning to cope with the rest of the world. And this is where Bhutan's Dragon King has tried to steer his tiny kingdom to, since the 1980s.

People here are proud of their human-centered development approach, an achievement seen through, among others, their program towards primary school enrolment for both boys and girls, and expanding rural health care system. Their people's well-being, therefore, is one those noncompromisable forms of wealth that Bhutanese leaders want to safeguard from the perils of embracing globalization too soon or too recklessly.

No other development perhaps best represents the mind-boggling impact of Bhutan's decision to open up to the world than its introduction to "box" or television and the Internet in mid-1999, when the King lifted a ban on TV as part of the events marking his Silver Jubilee on the throne. Later, the UNDP would help the government set up its first Internet system. As it turned out, such event would take place while I served as resident representative in the kingdom.

In my annual report for 2000 as resident coordinator, here is how I explained the significance of such developments:

"Interest in ICT was fueled in Bhutan by the introduction of the Internet in June 1999. A unique environment exists and greatly improves the chances for success of an information-enabled society; widespread knowledge of English; excellent telecommunications network in much of the country; small and relatively well-educated population; little previous computerization, allowing the adoption of new standards; manageable amount of data; and Government committed to adoption of ICT. Because of its landlocked geographic location, Bhutan's need for Information technology is large, as are the potential benefits. The establishment of ICT capacity in the districts is expected to contribute toward a comprehensive, coordinated information system. Transparency and accountability also can be enhanced. Indeed, ICT may prove the most significant catalyst in bringing development to rural areas."

The UNDP initiative was greatly boosted by a decision to focus on strengthening "multi-bi" cooperation with Japan through the Japanese Trust Fund. With this, it initiated a US$450,000 ICT Knowledge Project that would create local ICT technical capacity in four districts and a mega-data centre in Thimphu—the idea being to bridge the information gap between national and district administrations.

The UNV, which is also administered in Bhutan by the UNDP, provided seven volunteer ICT experts to the Government through a second project, also funded by Japan, for US$311,000. The UNDP also provided ICT exposure for the youth in Thimphu through the experimental and highly popular "Internet Café" programme and helped to strengthen and expand Druknet, the country's only Internet Service Provider.

The ICT program introduced by the UNDP quickly found applications in areas of governance and skills development projects. The information network for good governance supported the planning commission in its efforts to facilitate the decentralization process.

The schools were the next beneficiary of the ICT program, as UNICEF began to look at ICT applications for education. As part of efforts to familiarize students with the Internet and information technology, a new program was launched in the capital, a 1-to2-month-long program that provides them hands-on opportunity to explore various means of using computer-assisted research, among others.

In 2000, the UNDP started the Internet Café initiative, providing more than 1,300 students and unemployed youth with access to computer training and Internet in Timphu. We believed then that by making young high school graduates more IT-literate, we improve their chances of entering the workforce. We were also proud of the team of ICT specialists from the UN Volunteers.

The UNV specialists, for one, made an important contribution at Sherbtse College, the highest institution of learning in Bhutan; as well as youth centers and the Royal Institute of Management. They are the critical mass of ICT expertise which is helping Bhutan build its own technical capacity.

At the Ministry of Agriculture, another UV volunteer, Ed Santos, made a difference by helping create an information system to help the nation's farmers who represent 80 percent of the population.

"The Ministry of Agriculture recognizes the great potentials of IT in management and sustainable use of Bhutan's renewable natural resource . IT integration is in every aspect of the operationalization and institutionalization of every current program," says Santos.

Partnership being an integral part of our strategy, we sought the help of the government of Japan and the JOCV dispatched several volunteers to strengthen capacities for

ICT training.

UNDP felt honored by the way our government counterparts trusted us as a catalyst in ICT and communication.

One female teacher represents, meanwhile, the sense of ownership that the Bhutanese had with the national effort to wire the kingdom. "Before there were no computers in school. Now, teachers are given computer facilities which can update our knowledge and we can learn more things and pass them on to our students."

One female student chorused: "It's important for me to have computers. With the help of computers, everything has gone far. Everything is in the computer, so if I didn't learn computers, I won't be able to go, to do anything in the world."

Perhaps one other value of the Internet that we did not foresee immediately is that it now helps balance out the negative effects of TV's invasion. To be sure, young people can—and do—pick up a lot of garbage from the Internet, but since the schools have a definite ICT program, they can at least be guided in the use of technology, unlike with TV, which has been blamed in some quarters for its indiscriminate programming and the fact it has altered some of the time-honored family values and rituals in Bhutanese households.

The Bhutan Broadcasting Service (BBS), which the King had envisioned to take the lead in guiding his people in the age of TV, is facing stiff competition from foreign competition that many young Bhutanese find more appealing than the homegrown cultural programs on Buddhism, or the local news.

Within a matter of months after TV invaded Bhutan, "the Bhutanese wanted more than a locally produced reflection of themselves; they wanted the world—a 24-hour, 500-channel universe," according to one article posted on the Online edition of *Kuensel*.

"For a society that's trying to preserve its own culture and values, all this comes as a bit of a shock," the article quoted Kinley Dorji, Kuensel's editor, as lamenting.

Soon, young children were staying glued to MTV, to wrestling, and some such Western programs that could only further weaken efforts to preserve the Bhutanese spirituality.

This "battle" for the hearts and minds of the young Bhutanese is important, because its people are Bhutan's only line of defense, being sandwiched by India and China, with its physical defense buttressed only by some 6,000 soldiers.

As the article in the *Kuensel* online edition put it, the educational system, which has control of the children by day, is the main force countering any undue influence of the box at night. An estimated one fifth of the population is captive to the TV. Valued education has been given more attention the past two years, in the hope that the children can grow as model Buddhists, able to cope with the impact of globalization in all aspects.

And in this educational initiative, the school system relies heavily on the Internet.

The stiff competition posed by TV is explained in the *Kuensel* article as owing to the strong oral culture of the Bhutanese, which makes TV more appealing than typing in words and having to navigate through so much information on the Internet. But hopefully, this can change, as ICT applications are widened and the practice of computer-aided instruction becomes routine.

The ICT applications have supported the UN Country team's advocacy campaigns, which in turn were boosted also by our Bhutan Radio programme and the UN/Bhutan Forums. The impact of IT on Bhutan's national capacity building was driven home in the summation provided by Mr. Dasho Leki Dorji, Deputy Minister for Communications, at the Round Table Meeting in Thimphu in November, 2000, as well as in the technical presentation by Mr. Kinga Singye. Executive director of BBS.

He stressed the need to improve the programme content for both BBS and Bhutan Radio, in order to make them more appealing to the young, and then, eventually, to extend their coverage throughout the kingdom.

The RGOB expressed a hope of developing a vibrant IT industry with the potential to open up employment opportunities and export IT services. The government had created a new Division of Information Technology, and formulated an IT Master Plan.

Mr. Singye's presentation underscored the priorities of

developing adequate ICT infrastructure throughout the country, developing human resource capacities in the sector, Particularly in the Dzongkhags and the private sector, as well as in integrating IT into the educational system and adopting information management systems in state agencies. The private sector, in turn, will be entrusted with developing the computer support and software industry.

Beyond the cultural pros and cons of opening up Bhutan to the forces of globalization, the government acknowledged the economic advantages of preparing the country for competition. Mr. Achyut Bhandari, Director-General of the Department of Trade, listed at the RTM session the opportunities; greater access to global markets, expansion of trade and other links, foreign investment and transfer of technology, the potential for developing knowledge and technology-based industries, as well as that of improved economic efficiency and competitiveness, and employment generation.

One particular challenge of globalization that Bhutan had to face was its private sector, which accounted for only 15 percent of the total labor force. The private sector lacked the capital and other resources to finance large-scale investments. Growth was constrained by the daunting terrain and distance from markets, inadequate infrastructure, limited access to credit facilities, shortage of skilled manpower and lack of entrepreneurial and managerial capacity. It must be noted that much of these constraints could be eased along by wider and more creative

ICT applications, and this is why we gave that ICT development the highest priority while I was there.

ICT was also seen to play a key role in Bhutan's good governance efforts, which were roughly categorised under four interrelated themes; judicial and legislative reforms, human rights and human development, transparency and accountability, and participatory development and decentralisation. With the thrust on participatory development and decentralisation, it was important to find the most cost-efficient ways of applying ICT in order to strengthen the administrative and financial capacities of the dzongkhag or districts.

The rush to find ICT applications, however, comes up against the very real limitation of resources and capacities. Ms. Eimi Watanabe, who ably co-chaired the RTM, had advised a prioritisation of ICT needs, as she deemed the ICT master plan too ambitious as to require major investments that could not all be immediately secured. She highlighted two priorities that had recurred in discussions, i.e., the need to improve the quality of the socioeconomic database, and the need to enhance the revenue base, through broadening the tax base and user charges, in order to reduce dependency on aid.

Part of Bhutan's evolution into a modern, well-equipped society in the community of nations would eventually require its being weaned away from the tremendous levels of foreign aid it is now getting.

In that long journey, it must learn to continually look

inward into the deepest strengths of national character, while marching confidently onward, its eye cast on the tremendous opportunities for growth in a rapidly shrinking, highly competitive world. One of my fondest hopes is to see the ICT revolution we helped start serve it in good stead on that journey.

CHAPTER 11

MINDANAO REVISITED

While on vacation from school in the summer of 1973, then 14-year-old Mohammad Fhardi Adjimin took his oath of allegiance to the Parhimpunan Kabangsaan Anak Islam (PARKAI), an underground movement that served as a front for the Moro National Liberation Front.

His father was already very much involved in the Muslim secessionist war as a fighter and mass leader, inspiring the young Fhardi to undergo military training.

From a mere cadre, he emerged as the fourth state chairman of Palawan in 1994. Two years later the government forged a peace pact with the MNLF, changing the shape of the Muslim struggle in the south. Fhardi became part of the Human Resource Development Programme (HRDP) on leadership and government, which set into motion a capacity-building program to strengthen the capabilities of the Southern Philippine Council for Peace and Development (SPCPD).

The SPCPD was the government-created institution that would later involve the MNLF combatants and their families in finding a solution to the socioeconomic problems in the 14 cities and provinces where the Muslim secessionist campaign escalated. Fhardi considers the HRDP to be a program " which is very much concerned with the impact of the people." He is optimistic that the initiatives of linking the MNLF leadership and the Peace and Development Advocates (PDA) with other sectors of society constitute the right approach to postconflict community building.

The HRDP is also part of the SPCPD-NEDA-UN Multi-Donor Assistance Programme, which was initiated and continues to play a significant role in nurturing peace, while improving living conditions and capacities of MNLF combatants and their families.

Looking back, I'm convinced that while Mindanao may continue to emerge as troubled spot, the initiatives of both government and MNLF leaders have greatly influenced their thinking that a lasting peace can still be attained—even if it has to take one step at a time.

This is the same justification that impelled Fhardi and other ex-MNLF combatants to continue the development work in Mindanao despite growing threats from so-called Muslim extremists who, although small in number, have been making headlines due to their involvement in an escalation of violence and criminality in Mindanao, topped by the headline-grabbing spate of kidnappings.

To make things worse, parts of Mindanao continue to witness sporadic clashes involving certain MNLF ex-combatants, or the Moro Islamic Liberation Front (MILF), the breakaway Muslim secessionist movement that has emerged as the largest rebel fighting force in the south. The island is also perennially challenged by the banditry of so-called pseudo-Islamic groups such as the Abu Sayyaf that have borrowed the mantle of religious crusades to carry out senseless crimes.

Confidence building from both sides is important considering the fragile status of the peace pact. The best illustration of such fragility is that, even as this book was being updated, Mr. Misuari was clamped in jail, facing rebellion charges for his men's attack on a Jolo army detachment after he alleged tried to renew calls for rebellion. More than a hundred people died in the Jolo raid and in the standoff at a government complex in Zamboanga City, with Misuari loyalists, dubbed "Misuari Renegade Group" by the military, being blamed for the mess.

Although he was elected governor of the Autonomous Region in Muslim Mindanao, Misuari's last few months in office had been marred with charges of corruption. He was eventually replaced as MNLF chairman by a 15-man committee, and the MNLF decided to support the candidacy of Parouk Hussin, a central committee member and MNLF foreign relations chief, to run in the ARMM gubernatorial elections.

Despite the fate that befell Misuari, the MNLF continues to transform its "peace zones" into full-fledged economic zones. The government, on the other hand, continues to pursue peace initiatives with the MILF. The prospects for peace remain strong.

The Organization of Islamic Conference, meanwhile, recognized the new government in the ARMM—in what was taken as a signal that it was accepting the political structure of the Bangsa Moro people in Mindanao. Misuari's successor, ARMM Gov. Parouk Hussin, is now overseeing a new range of development projects in Mindanao, although he claimed in his inaugural speech he inherited from his predecessor less than 500,000 Peso in cash and accounts payable of 22 million Peso.

In June 2002, the MNLF leadership affirmed despite the fallout between the government and the Misuari group, it still recognizes the 1996 peace agreement and has no plans of dropping it.

The multidonor progamme, on the other hand, has entered the third phase,titled, "Strengthening the Foundations of Lasting Peace and Development in the Southern Philippines." This was anchored on strengthening the trust and confidence established among major stakeholders as well as strengthening community-based management of productive capacities.

According to UN documents in Manila, the program addresses current challenges to peace and development, including:

- **Meaningful autonomy under the new law.** When the third phase was being drawn up, the outcome of the ARMM plebiscite was still being deliberated upon by the Philippine legislature and until such time that it was passed, there were uncertainties over the powers to be vested in the new regional autonomous government. When the plebiscite was held on August 14, 2001, the island province of Basilan and Marawi—the only Islamic City in the country—finally joined Maguindanao, Lanao del Sur, Sulu and Tawi-Tawi in the ARMM.
- **Perceived lack of national government visibility.** There was a perceived absence of a clearly defined government commitment in the peace and development effort, and even the existing contributions of government were poorly recognized by the stakeholders. Most stakeholders accept the need for additional assistance, but with more than a 90 billion Peso deficit, the government is hard-pressed to carry out the interventions. However, there remain efforts to increase allocations to Mindanao. At the Mindanao Budget Summit in 1999, the Medium-Term Public Investment Program showed an increase from 5.97 billion Peso in 1999 to 7.96 billion Peso in 2000 for Mindanao. The national budget also showed an increase from 45.2 billion Peso in 2000 to 10.7 billion Peso for 2001. Private sector investment, however, remains limited, given concerns over peace and order despite Mindanao's being considered a potentially productive area.

- **Weak institutional and human resource capacity.** The weak human base of the SPCPD and the ARMM affected their ability to mobilize and coordinate the agencies under their supervision. Relatedly, weak financial accounting compounded the lack of technical and management skills, and affected the national government's level and timeliness of fund releases.
- **Complex and institutional arrangements.** Decision-making on SZOPAD was deemed to be "quite complex" with three regional development councils, the ARMM government covering four provinces, the Mindanao Economic and Development Council (Medco) the Office of the Presidential Assistants for Regional Concerns (Pareco), SPCPD and its 81-person Consultative Assembly and the Cabinet Supervisory Committee to oversee the implementation of the 1996 GRP-MNLF peace agreement, and the Mindanao Coordinating Council.
- **Widespread perception of patronage and corruption on all sides.** Installing mechanisms for clear and transparent reporting on the use of funds could improve this perception. Monitoring and supervision undertaken by the SPCPD with donors needed to be enhanced.
- **Moving away from exclusivity.** There was a widely shared agreement within the MNLF and government that MNLF members or former combatants should not only be the program focus. Muslims, Christians and the "Lumads" who share similar problems of isolation and

unmet basic human needs should also participate on the basis of need.
- **Unmet, unrealistic expectations.** In an area where few regular government programs were available, MNLF expectations of major peace additionality had not been met. Achieving more "regular" program coverage of the entire SZOPAD area by local government units would be a major and desirable change.
- **Healing old wounds and social fractures.** The conflict and its causes were not easily forgotten. The stakeholders continue to need education about the peace process and help in learning nonviolent and effective techniques of conflict resolution and cultural coexistence.
- **Continuing armed conflict between the Armed Forces and the Moro Islamic Liberation Front.** The continued armed struggle of the MILF for an Islamic state poses a major threat to the stability of the region. Unfortunately, the MILF has also presented itself as a fallback for disgruntled MNLF rebels who were unable to participate in or benefit from the various measures of reintegration; and who may perceive the government to be insincere; or their leaders to be ineffective in representing their interests. Strengthening the current peace agreement with the MNLF presents a better alternative to armed conflict.

The third phase of the multi-donor program is geared towards improving the capacities of target communities in partnership with their local governments to ensure self-sustaining development and improved access to basic services. Despite political differences between some local government executives and MNLF commanders, the Mindanao experiment on peace and development showed that forging partnerships was the most effective medium to reach down to the grassroots level.

Eight components were included in the third phase, namely; capacity building and empowerment through peace and development communities, building partnerships and strengthening institutional support mechanisms, special emergency response and relief, improved access to basic services, community enterprise and entrepreneurship development in nonfarm sector, sustainable livelihood development, confidence building through advocacy and promotion of a culture of peace and programme management and coordination.

At least 150 Peace and Development Councils (PDCs) have emerged to manage and monitor development programs and reconstruction work in MNLF areas. The Peace and Development Advocates, who are actually MNLF combatants or zone commanders, serve as catalysts and community mobilizers for the program with the support of national UN volunteers.

To strengthen the capacity of key institutions as well as institutional mechanisms of governance for sustained peace-building and development in Mindanao, a common framework was drawn up for the implementation and policy dialogues with government partners at the regional and sub regional levels of the program.

For all the best intentions of all parties involved in the third phase of the multidonor programme, however, new developments have emerged which could complicate peace and development. As is well known, the United States, with full backing by the Philippine government, has assumed a very strong presence in Mindanao since the September 11 terrorist attacks in Washington and New York.

The declared intention was for the US forces to train Philippine troops in fighting terrorist groups, topped by the Abu Sayyaf. While no US troops were to be involved in direct combat, concern was lately raised over whether the increased American presence and the Philippine government's acquiescence in a more aggressive campaign accused in some areas of riding roughshod over human rights might not serve to fuel the tension, especially in Muslim-dominated areas.

A handful of designated Peace and Development Communities had already been casualties in the all-out war declared by the military against the MILF during the Estrada administration. Some of these PDCs were accidentally shelled by the military, and it is to the credit of the parties holding up the peace agreement that the MNLF state chairmen with jurisdiction over these PDCs peacefully settled the matter with the military brass.

With the US-backed Arroyo administration's aggressive campaign, however, already complaints of arbitrary arrests have surfaced. In one celebrated case, a tribal woman accused an American soldier of joining a Philippine military raid on a village in Basilan, and then shooting a villager tagged as suspected Abu Sayyaf member. Tensions like this have often put former MNLF leaders in a bind, wishing to provide quick response to crisis and yet trying to avoid reviving confrontations with the military.

Indeed, the Mindanao situation remains tricky as ever, and will likely remain so for much longer. As the continuing impact of September 11 is felt, many parts of the South will feel caught in the crossfire of a state needing to ensure security and of rebels needing to negotiate the best terms from the government.

CHAPTER 12

A BETTER MAP FOR CHANGING TERRAIN

Peace before development; seen through this prism, Mindanao seems in some ways a microcosm of what is happening worldwide.

If I have been undergoing a long, arduous, internal struggle for change, trying to set new directions for myself and my career, the institution I work for—the United Nations—stands even more challenged.

Since the origins of the Bretton Woods system, no single issue has so galvanized international public opinion on the issue of how nations should live among themselves, for their mutual survival—or, conversely, destruction—as the Asian financial crisis which threatened to engulf both worlds of the poor and the rich as I was writing the first edition of this book.

What first began as a flu among the miracle economies of East Asia has affected many other regions of the globe, compelling attention to what was hitherto a taken-for-granted risk; the unbridled capital flows and the kind of economic religion that motivated them.

Since then, in a short span of three years, the world was further shaken up by a continually rising crescendo of protests over the inequitable global economic system, an arrangement seen as being perpetuated by the multilateral institutions that had arisen out of the second world war, chiefly represented by the International Monetary Fund, the World Bank, and more recently, the World Trade Organisation. From Seattle to Genoa to Prague, the protests grew more violent, the voices for change more aggressive.

If there was any doubt about the urgency of the reforms they demanded—regardless of the protesters' tactics—such doubt was erased completely by the September 11 terrorist attacks on the United States.

Beyond being a purely violent reaction to the centuries of inequities between North and South, and between the rich, industrial West and the developing world, 9/11 became a wake-up call to leaders to find the roots of deep unrest, albeit without justifying the resort to terrorism.

The Human Development Report for 2001, underscoring the need to deepen democracy at the global, quoted British Prime Minister Tony Blair's first reactions to 9/11: "Our illusion has been shattered on September 11; that we can have the good life of the West irrespective of the state of the rest of the world....The dragon's teeth are planted in the fertile soil of wrongs unrighted, of disputes left to fester for years, of failed states, of poverty and deprivation."

I would rather, however, look at this series of crisis as an opportunity, a blessing in disguise, so to speak, that helps people realize more clearly the implications of living without that certain critical balance that is required in everything we do—as reflected in growth without equity, in unsustainable development, in unmanaged globalization, among others.

For the past decades, the activists in the United Nations have forced people to stand up and notice what has been going on in the world; to challenge the pat, convenient interpretations of what was going on in countries both rich and poor as well as the formulaic solutions that experts have come up with; and to make some bold assertions and advance visions that at first seemed impossible but are now clearly attainable.

In my view, one of the most important of such changes was the emergence of the concept of human development, and subsequently, of sustainable human development. For years, academics and the more prescient of development workers have advocated putting a human face to the formulas swallowed by many countries that had structural adjustment programs with the IMF and its twin, the World Bank. But this pushing-the-frontiers attitude took an irreversible turn when a panel of international development experts, led by Mahbub Ul-haq, the then advisor to the UNDP administrator, advanced the human development paradigm in the late 1980s. It could not have happened later, for the 80s had been called "the lost decade" and if the changes had not taken place then, it would have compromised the future and well-being of even more generations.

In 1990, the UNDP published the first of what would be a yearly Human Development Report. That pathbreaking report advocated enlarging people's choices with regard to their economic and social well-being and introduced the Human Development Index (HDI), a composite measure of a people's life expectancy, literacy, and income. It would later be complemented by the Gender Empowerment Measure, the Gender-oriented Development Index and the Human Poverty Index.

The UNDP's Human Development Reports have attained a certain relevance because they have bravely tackled some of the most difficult tests for development planners and workers in our time—the impact of globalization, women, and poverty, consumption patterns in rich and poor countries, and the promotion of rights in multicultural societies, among others. The most recent HDR, "Deepening Democracy in a Fragmented Report," is a must read for those who take development work and its links to politics and economics seriously. It is a brutally frank assessment of how inequities have been allowed to fester, by sins of omission and commission, in UN member states and in the global setting. It is the best argument for why the UN must guarantee the independence of such a report, thus allowing the multinational team led by Dr. Sakiko Fukuda-Parr the leeway necessary to explain problems in an atmosphere of candor and in the spirit of critical collaboration.

Subsequently, country HDRs have been done in certain countries like the Philippines, where a Human Development Network became the UNDP's partner in advocacy work. So far, more than 400 country and regional reports have been produced—a rich harvest indicating an irreversible march to progress—not only in terms of human development, but also in terms of progress in promoting transparency and accountability among governments and their partners. One of the most talked-about regional reports is the one produced for the Arab League, which has lifted the veil on some of the darkest corners of inequity—especially gender inequities and injustice—in some Muslim societies.

The concept of a sustainable human development could not have come at a more opportune time. In fact, if it had come a little later, I fear that it would have been too late.

Now, more than ever, events such as the Asian crisis, 9/11 and the continuing impact of globalization have jolted rich and poor alike into seeing the folly of a development path that is either too narrowly growth-oriented or too locked into austerity measures, or one that is anchored on a misleading kind of macroeconomic growth sustained by unregulated capital movements.

Today, as the former UNDP Administrator James Gustav Speth has so boldly put it, the world needs "a new architecture for development cooperation." Addressing the National Press Club in Washington, D.C. in October 1998, Mr. Speth said the UN's challenge is to make globalization work for human development and for people. Unless this is done, the backlash from concerned sectors could threaten the process (of globalization) itself.

The call for a new framework for development cooperation comes with specific shifts and reforms, as outlined by Mr. Speth.

1) First, broaden development cooperation to include not only development assistance but also trade and capital flows. The strictly government-to-government cooperation of the past must be done away with.

The inclusion of trade and capital flows in the development cooperation framework becomes critical in the aftermath of the Asian crisis, which illustrated how all the supposed economic and social gains achieved by the miracle economies of East Asia were swept away in one blow when the trade and capital flows, which quickened with globalization, were not managed and therefore their impact was not predicted.

Meanwhile, according to Mr. Speth, it is time as well to do away withthe "convenient concoctions" that have guided past action. These are the myths that:

a) globalization is doing well
b) the crisis is easing up
c) trade and private capital are reliable substitutes for development assistance and
d) progress can depend entirely on the wisdom of the market.

We also need a fundamental redefinition of relationships between rich and poor countries. Mr. Speth is prompted to ask the question: Does this world of underdevelopment and poverty really matter to a rich, stable country like the US, for instance, which "all too often behaves as if the world didn't matter"? Can the world of the 3 billion people in poverty (or at least, the 1.3 billion who subsist on $1 a day) matter to the very rich? Yes, it can, it must, for the sake of the rich themselves. A backlash against such highly inequitable divisions of the world's resources can impact on the very rich, as experience has shown.

The UNDP's Poverty Report of 1998 notes that the assets of three billionaire American equals the total GDP of 50 countries.

2) Second, we need a new development framework to consolidate the developing concept of sustainable development.

3) Third, we all need to learn from past mistakes, and ensure that development cooperation supports polity, not

just government. Mr. Speth notes how governance has become a big issue in development cooperation—improving basic capacities of governments; rebuilding judicial systems; overhauling land claims systems.

4) Fourth, development assistance must be sharply increased.

Development assistance is now at an all-time low, says the 1998 Poverty Report, which warns that we will all pay for this neglect.

The US, for instance, has kept its development assistance levels at constantly lower levels even while its economy improved through the years. In 1956, the US accounted for 63 percent of all development assistance in the world. In 1997, that ratio was down to only 13 percent. Among OECD countries, the "US is dead last" as contributor to development aid, notes Mr. Speth. Yet the US has the greatest stake, the one that stands most to benefit, from globalization; logically, it should be the top supporter of an economic interdependence among nations.

One of the most eloquent explanations for the raison de'etre of development cooperation is provided by Mr. Speth: For decades, he said, most rich countries and multilateral institutions justified development assistance " in the context of fighting communism or [promoting] human rights." But the Nordic countries did not require that kind of justification. "They saw development assistance as basically the price one must pay to live in a world of civilization norms... to feel good about oneself."

To be fair, the UN has pushed steadily forward, since the first 1990 Human Development Report, to promote a new "architecture" for development cooperation. The reforms have quickened with the entry of Mr. Kofi Annan as secretary general.

Over the past two years, we have been guided by what is called the UNDAF (for UN development assistance framework), which mandates all UN agencies to work more closely together, pooling very, very scarce resources and coordinating initiatives so as to maximize their impact.

This new framework has been adopted alongside an internal change process in the UN—we have seen a downsizing and reengineering; more accountability; and cost-cutting.

The changes in the UN have clearly been reflected in the UNDP, which is now the world's biggest multilateral source of grant assistance (it manages $2 billion annually).

It was in 1965 when the UNDP's role as a funding agency first grew and the UN specialised agencies started to undertake particular concerns—UNESCO for education, FAO for agriculture, etc. At that time, the UNDP was not yet seen as the kind of knowledge-based, experience-based, capacity and HRD-promoting organization at all. That was the time when we were labeled as simply a funding agency, the largest dispenser of grant assistance in the world.

But the dynamics have changed now. The specialized agencies no longer have a monopoly of expertise in their areas. We now encourage NGOs and private groups to work with us, to enrich the work of the UN people.

The UNDP's coordinating role within the UN has also recently come to the fore. Lyn Pieper of AusAid thinks that happened with our experience in Mindanao after the 1996 peace agreement. This is the first time, she recalls, "that I've seen the UNDP make a major effort to coordinate, and play its role in its area of expertise which is social and community development."

From the Australian viewpoint, she says, channeling the assistance for Mindanao through UNDP was but logical: " The UNDP has a mandate to decide how the fund will be used, and then we expect the UNDP to keep us informed always regarding the progress of outcomes. Where did the money go? What happened? Did it work?"

Lyn's pitch for coordinated assistance couldn't be any clearer or bolder: "We believed that peace-building and donor involvement would not work, unless all the donors are coordinated, because the SPCPD, the Muslims in Mindanao, had neither government nor NGO structures. There was nothing there that would allow them to cope with every single donor coming in separately. So we were very keen that they had to deal with one group, not all of us."

I believe the UNDP must continue extending affirmative action for the needy. Working with the UNDP should primarily mean helping the weaklings, the disadvantaged countries and marginalized people. The UN system at large is designed to help the weakest nations. That's the difference between the World Bank and the UN system—although now, after the Asian crisis, even the World Bank has acknowledged the need to challenge previous capitalist orthodoxy and to lend more focus to sustainable human development.

This is affirmed by no less than the current UNDP Administrator, Mr. Mark Malloch Brown, who as former vice president of the World Bank had the opportunity to look at both the UNDP's and the Bank's missions. Sustainable human development has apparently won the day, Mr. Brown gladly asserts, and further points to the increasing demand for UNDP support for good governance initiatives as an indication that political leaders and their private-sector partners acknowledge the key role of politics in defining and carrying out development policies. Economics and markets are important, he says, "but the big lesson of the period is never ignore the critical of politics in allowing people to shape their own lives. Political development is the forgotten dimension of human development."

Part of the UNDP's mandate is to promote the capabilities of LDCs. We are trying to bring the LDCs people into the picture, showing them that peace and development is the real basis for the UN system.

Actually, if one comes right down to it, peace and development was the original motivation behind setting up the UN. We should go back to that.

Lyn Pieper has a word of caution there, though; post-conflict resolution, she says, is very complicated, and peacebuilding as a development process is equally complicated. This fact all the more underscores, in her view, why that kind of process, such as what we had in Mindanao, should be done through the UN system.

The UNDP is, meanwhile, also taking the lead in programs developing governance. It is one clear indication, in Lyn's view, that the UNDP is trying to find a niche where it can add value in a way that other donors cannot.

In the past several years, civil society has played an increasing role in making things happen. Government itself is no longer just the prominent agent for solving people's problems; its role has diminished. Therefore, we have to look for a sound partnership with the civil society, or the private sector.

Even the issue of human rights is more of a governance issue.

This means: The government is supposed to be doing what its Constitution mandates. For sure, a number of governments have violated the constitutions of their countries in more ways than one.

This paradox isn't really surprising, for within the UN set-up itself, we find even greater paradoxes. The entire UN system preaches democracy, it deploys massive resources to countries trying to make the change from dictatorships to democracy, and wastes no time exerting moral suasion, if possible, on regimes that violate their people's human rights. Yet within the UN itself, we have a virtual dictatorship by the Group of 5—the five permanent members of the UN Security Council.

As long as the veto powers by superpowers are there, we will be overruled. The matter of the very limited voting rights in the UN was elaborated on in this year's Human development Report, which frankly stated that if democracy is to be deepened globally in order to arrest the continuing fragmentation in the world, the first place to do so is the UN.

You see the General Assembly particularly for the political veto powers, not development veto powers. If you ask me, we don't have to [give] any of those five countries this so-called privilege. The ideal way of looking at it is to give each vote an equal voice. That way, we can ensure an inner voice can be heard from developing countries.

The grant of unparalleled powers and authority to an elite group was justified, after the second world war, by the overarching need to maintain peace in the world, so the development can follow. But so many things have happened since then, and the times call for giving the little countries—whose names we like to invoke—a real voice in the UN. Perhaps, as we carry the tenets of good governance to others, calling for democratization, market reforms, an end to corruption, better justice systems, we in the UN would do well to reflect on our own state of governance. I am sure we will find some good things, and a lot of bad. But that is how development workers are supposed to look at themselves and their work—with a clinical eye, objectively ferreting out valid observations from hunches and speculations, constantly finding out how the world can be made a little bit better.

CHAPTER 13

Homeland and New Horizons

In my dealings, in my relations, I am always direct. In my career I always want to go forward, reach father.... But my life seems to be a series of desires and situations that meander and twist, eventually coming full circle.

Coming back to Japan, I felt anxiety and excitement were tangled up in my mind, coupled with cultural shock after 20 years. For me, after Bhutan, I want to become a trainer for development administration in Japan. Now I became a university professor, working with university students, and inspiring them to do a development work. University professor was not exactly I have planned out to become.

But, doing this academic job in Japan, where there seems to me a dearth of such trainers, I become a practitioner in a different sense. I hold seminars, and bring my students to Mindanao or elsewhere to let them see the reality of the people who are living under the very difficult circumstances. In my own way, I want to return what has been my country's as well as UN's investment in me, and make my own personal, professional, and emotional investment in the younger generations.

I would of course continue my advocacy work, of which I consider this book to be an integral part. I would like to see a greater development involvement by the Japanese mass media, NGOs, civil society, academia, and perhaps morality organizations. I might go around as a workshop trainer, and lecturer; I may continue to write and share my insights and thoughts.

It is indeed a continuing process, a continuing challenge to existing values. If development workers were just meant to be preservationists, then I would not be thinking this way.

Such an attitude of questioning, probing and improving—ensures constant progress. I am not talking about imagery or physical terms, but thinking terms. We always need do try to do something about what is going on, to remove the fear of the issues, and involve ourselves in real problem solving through human relations. This is something UN can do better than anyone else.

I consider all these will be a very long-term, but nonetheless challenging assignments. They need the type of people in Japanese society. Is this the reason why I came back to Japan to raise the younger generation? In fact, I came back to Japan because of my family; my wife Hiroko was diagnosed as breast cancer; Kei has reached his age to go to the elementary school, considered to be a critical period for Japanese education; and aging Hiroko' parents would expect us to return to Japan sooner rather than later.

Given a promotion opportunity to go back to UNDP HQ, I turned it down and chose family and this time, absolutely, my family came first. This is somewhat most of development workers tend to make a mistake to choose career. I would not forget how much my family and the relatives supported me during my career of UN. My son also put up with hardships, eating a lot of canned foods, who could not taste real ice-cream, tender beef, etc. Hiroko is recovering from the breast cancer though she needs more time to adjust her life style.

Still Hiroko shares my own sense of dynamism and excitement at how things can change. As she reflected back on my development career, she told me: "Although it's really hard life, it's very interesting to see the change of a country. It's very dynamic. I understand why you wanted to stay in development work. I understand that very well." Difficult as the journey has been for her, she remains my most staunch and wonderful partner.

I have loved her for her strength of character; she has loved me for my passion and commitment to serve people. She cannot imagine me without those. And I cannot imagine being in a place without people to associate with.

My journey as a development worker would continue to evolve, respecting value of my family support exploring potentials of human resources in development arena, and creating forum for development workers in Japan.

Perhaps till my dying days, I will be mingling with different personalities, and different cultures.

Nevertheless, my spirit to serve vulnerable people would not change: I could hear inside of me, saying "I can go anywhere, everywhere. Just as long as there are people there."

Appendix

緊急援助と開発協力のはざまから
―開発ワーカーのディレンマ

人間らしい生き方を求めて地球的視野からの活動

（ＧＬＭインスティチュート設立記念基調講演サマリー）

　国連開発計画（UNDP）で20年余り、特にアジア・アフリカ（ウガンダ、エチオピア、南スーダン、中国、モンゴル、フィリピン：ミンダナオ島平和交渉 focal point、ブータン―常駐代表、等）を中心に緊急援助も含めた紛争・社会問題関連のプロジェクトに従事した。その職務経験を踏まえて国際紛争の形態とそれに関連する援助政策の研究を進めると同時に、国際教育の観点から、社会の民主化と平和の実現を希求する上で、21世紀に求められている開発ワーカーとは何かを考えていきたい。
　そのような動機から今回の基調講演は、非常に型破りの聴衆に呼びかける方式で、開発ワーカーのディレンマを三つのカテゴリーに分けて紹介した。

１．開発理論のディレンマ
　学問的には、紛争や貧困（従属変数）の因果関係（独裁政権、排他的文化、構造的差別、貧富の差、等）―― ROOT CAUSE（原因の源）となる因子（独立変数）を見極めつつ、政策科学の分野で問題解決のための政策を具体化し、被援助国コミュニティーのニーズに応じたプロジェクトを効果的に、かつ効率的に立案し、迅速に実行されなければならない。果たしてこのような理想が現実には可能なのであろうか。そして、援助国側の調整介入――

ADJUSTED INTERVENTION（基調講演者の NEW WORD）はカンボジア、アフガニスタン、イラク、東チモール、等の GOVERNANCE プロジェクト（選挙や政治のシステムも含めて）において表面化しており、条件付の ODA はもはや内政干渉のボーダーラインを超えているようにも映る。被援助国の自助努力とは裏腹に、依存を長引かせる要因は援助される側はもとより援助する側にも説明責任が問われてもいいのではないだろうか。最近の開発援助は GOVERNANCE のコンセプトを BUILT-IN させた「協調・調整介入型」が目立ってきた。自助努力を念頭に置いた CAPACITY BUILDING のプロジェクトは複雑かつ流動的で、時間もかかるが、社会インフラの基礎を築くためには、この分野の研究は奨励されるべきであろう。

2．実践のディレンマ

　PCM（立案・審査・形成・実施・モニタリング／評価）は政策を具体的なプロジェクトで説明するには効果的な方法ではあるが、人道援助や緊急援助の場合、時間的な制約、条件付の ODA、援助調整の難しさ、等を考慮すると住民参加型プロジェクトの精神とは反対に、援助国の ODA 機関では大体人道援助の内容の青写真は出来上がっていて、現地の要請を微調整した形で、実施が始まるのが現状であろう。援助される側もリーダーの利権問題や、プロジェクトを実施するうえで組織の CAPACITY や人材不足が、かえって援助の依存度を助長する傾向にある（筆者のアフリカ経験から）。ここでさらに問題になるのは、緊急援助から復興援助、中・長期的援助に移行する変遷期に住民参加型プロジェクトへの実質的な移行をどのように、どういったペース配分で行われるのか検討されなければならない（援助のペース配分を誤ると、政治・社会不安を招く。筆者の初期のモンゴル行政・経済改革の経験、現在の東チモールの問題）。

1）援助国（国際機関は多年度予算を制度化している）の ODA 単年度予算制度の問題（今年のプロジェクト予算は、次の年には繰り越すことは不可）は現場のニーズにマッチしたプロジェクト INPUT の調整を困難に

している。途上国では、国家予算の30％以上ODAに依存している政府、Least Developing Countriesは少なくない。自国の予算とODAを連動させて管理するシステムが曖昧なため、腐敗や汚職を招きかねない。ここにおいても、協調・調整介入型のガバナンスのプロジェクトが案件として浮上してきている。

2）パートナーシップの複雑化（被援助国、援助国、国際機関、NGO／NPO、メディア、民間、研究機関、等のパートナーシップは複雑多岐にわたり、互いに競争し、なかなか援助の調整が効率的・効果的に進まない（フィリピン―ミンダナオ島のPOST-CONFLICT PEACE BUILDINGプロジェクトはUNが援助調整を効果的に導いた成功例）。又、援助機関それぞれが定期的報告書を作成する際、被援助国にとって大変な重荷であり、こういったPROGRESS REPORTの一本化も検討されている（ブータン王国はNATIONAL EXECUTION MANNUALを作成して、プロジェクト進行状況の報告書を一本化する傾向にある）。

3）メディアは人道援助中心にドラマチックに報道するため世界の世論の関心は人道援助にとかく集中し、それによって世界世論を心理的に、中・長期的開発プロジェクトを軽視する傾向に導いているのではないか。自助努力を促すCAPACITYの構築は、復興援助から中・長期的開発プロジェクトに移行するプロセスで徐々に高揚していく。このプロセスが特に重要で、国家開発計画のマスタープランに"住民の声"がどの程度反映されているか、開発援助における報道のあり方と報道の持続性を問われるべきではないか。

5）参加型プロジェクトはリーダーシップと民意の質・参加度の関連性をモニタリングし、プロジェクト実施期間中に、変化する環境に応じて民意の推移を調整しながらプロジェクトを軌道修正すべきである（技術的にはプロジェクトの修正は可能であっても、実行していないのが現状）。

6）評価においては、誰のための評価なのか、その教訓がどのようにしてプロジェクトの修正や次世代プロジェクトに生かされるのか、生かされて

きたのか、評価の情報公開・透明性はどうなのか。評価の情報公開は教訓——LEARNING EXPERIENCE を次世代プロジェクトに生かすため、積極的にデータベースを SHARE することが必要。

NOTE：このセクションでは、技術移転の時間的差異、異文化コミュニケーション等、上記に関連する人材育成の問題は重要とされながらも、時間的な制約のため十分討論ができなかったが、「提言」の部分で関連提案として列挙してみた。

3．生活面のディレンマ

　仕事は危険で、過酷で、風土病（マラリア、肝炎、等）にかかるのは日常茶飯事で、それでも黙々と仕事をこなしていく。開発ワーカーは、心のどこかで自分の仕事が、「誰かの役に立っている」と思っているのだろうか。いままで経験したことのないような人間と人間との触れ合いから生まれる同胞意識、感動、JOB SATISFACTION、生きがい、満足感。自己満足といわれようとも、それが自分に与えられた使命と信じて、全力で仕事に励む。しかし、このような過酷な仕事は、「いつまで続けることができるのだろうか」という不安が再三再度襲ってきて、病気になると、その気持ちはもっと現実的なものになる。家族は、開発援助——「人助け」の「亡霊」に捕りつかれている父や母を見て、困惑するばかりで、「安定した生活設計はもはやこの世界には存在し得ないのだろうか」と感じている。他人を助けるのにあれほど一生懸命だが、家庭には時間を作れない矛盾した状況は、不幸にも家族離散という最悪の結果を招くこともある。リスクが高く、金銭的にもそれほど魅力的でないこの職業に情熱を注ぐのは、何がそうさせるのであろうか。種々の活動を通して人間の尊厳を確かめ合い、人間が人間らしい生き方を求めている環境の中で精一杯働きたい。そこに尽きるのではないだろうか。開発ワーカーの生活は理想と現実がぶつかり合う「人間ドラマ」そのものと言えないだろうか。

(提言)
日本 ODA の政策関連
1) ODA 戦略の充実（外交政策関連性――各省庁との調整も含む）
    ・包括的ワークショップを通じて NICHE・比較優位性を明確にする
    ・現地事務所の強化――権限委譲
    ・ODA 多年度予算の実施
    ・DYNAMIC PROGRAMMING：環境の変化に応じ、柔軟性のある、プロジェクト修正が迅速にできる管理体制の早期構築
    ・ADOVOCACY――包括的な予算も必要だが、各プロジェクトに予算を BUILT-IN する
2) HIGH PROFILE HIGH RISK プロジェクトへの参加

    GOVERNANCE タイプのプロジェクトへの参加：選挙、地方自治体の強化、警察機構の近代化、裁判所の改革、公務員改革、会計検査院の強化、難民問題、国会・議会運営、等は協調・調整介入型の比較的リスクの高いプロジェクトであり、この種のプロジェクトは、国連との援助協調が望ましい。

パートナーシップと LEARNING NETWORK
1) プロジェクトの BEST PRACTICE ――評価も含む：データベースの構築――（GLM インスティテュートは開発教育の教材を開発）
2) PCM を利用し、COMPLEX PROGRAMMING のワークショップを充実させる（紛争関連、社会インフラ、ガバナンス、環境、ジェンダー、等を含む）

人材育成
1) 国際公共政策に携わる HUMAN CAPITAL の構築

    日本学生海外協力隊 (Japanese Student Overseas Cooperation Volunteer) の設立。ODA プロジェクトへの研修・ボランティア参加を促進。

2）開発援助教育に従事するトレーナーをトレーニングする TRAINING FOR TRAINER のプログラムを開発する
3）現地のプロジェクトリーダーの質（COMPLEX PROGRAMMING の熟知）を高揚するためのリーダーシップトレーニングを実施
4）TV で"YOUTH VOLUNTEER の語り場"をシリーズで放映する

(2003 年 1 月 29 日　東京 WOMEN'S PLAZA にて)

※国連の活動内容、組織、略号などについては http://www.unic.or.jp/ を参照されたい。

村田俊一　むらたしゅんいち

1953年福岡県生まれ。
76年関西学院大学法学部政治学科卒業後、82年にジョージワシントン大学院博士課程修了後、外務省より国連開発計画(UNDP)の日本人初めてのJPO(Junior Professional Officer)の一人として、ウガンダ、南スーダン、モンゴル、フィリピン、ブータンなどで20年勤務。2002年より関西学院大学総合政策学部教授。専攻：国際関係論・国際機構論及び国際紛争とその援助政策。

(USA, 1980)

Journey of a Development Worker

2003年5月20日初版第一刷発行

著　者　　村田　俊一
発行者　　山本　栄一
発行所　　関西学院大学出版会
所在地　　〒662-0891　兵庫県西宮市上ケ原1番町1-155
電　話　　0798-53-5233

印　刷　　協和印刷株式会社

© Shun-ichi Murata 2003
Printed in Japan by Kwansei Gakuin University Press
ISBN:4-907654-47-2
乱丁・落丁本はお取り替えいたします。
http://www.kwansei.ac.jp/press/